# LEADING WOMEN

# Princess Diana

Royal
Activist and
Fashion Icon

## CONSTANCE BEAUREGARDE

Cavendish Square
New York

Published in 2017 by Cavendish Square Publishing, LLC
243 5th Avenue, Suite 136, New York, NY 10016

Website: cavendishsq.com

Library of Congress Cataloging-in-Publication Data

Names: Beauregarde, Constance, author.
Title: Princess Diana : royal activist and fashion icon / Constance
Beauregarde.
Description: New York : Cavendish Square Pub., 2016. | Series: Leading
women | Includes bibliographical references and index.
Identifiers: LCCN 2016002178 (print) | LCCN 2016002534 (ebook) | ISBN
9781502619877 (library bound) | ISBN 9781502619884 (ebook)
Subjects: LCSH: Diana, Princess of Wales, 1961-1997--Juvenile literature. |
Princesses--Great Britain--Biography--Juvenile literature.
Classification: LCC DA591.A45 B43 2016 (print) | LCC DA591.A45 (ebook) | DDC
941.085092--dc23
LC record available at http://lccn.loc.gov/2016002178

Editorial Director: David McNamara
Editor: Elizabeth Schmermund
Copy Editor: Rebecca Rohan
Art Director: Jeffrey Talbot
Designer: Stephanie Flecha
Production Assistant: Karol Szymczuk
Photo Research: J8 Media

Printed in the United States of America

# CONTENTS

# CHAPTER ONE

# *Growing Up a Lady*

Princess Diana was one of the most powerful female icons of the twentieth century. Beloved by millions worldwide, she was known as "the people's princess" for her charming public persona and commitment to charity work. Throughout her lifetime, she transformed the idea of what it meant to be a princess, and at the time of her death the world mourned her as one would a personal friend. Her life story has been told countless times, each with differing accounts as to her happiness, health, and well-being. Regardless of the story's approach, there has been a passionate desire

Diana, Princess of Wales

to try and understand the woman who was Princess of Wales. On the eve of her funeral, Queen Elizabeth II put it best:

*No one who knew Diana will ever forget her. Millions of others who never met her, but felt they knew her, will remember her. I for one believe there are lessons to be drawn from her life and from the extraordinary and moving reaction to her death. I share in your determination to cherish her memory.*

Princess Diana was an extraordinary woman who led an inspiring life. But, as the queen suggested, the reason why so many people mourned her as if she were a personal friend was because she was relatable. For many nonroyals, Diana was just like them. And, in a way, she was.

## Born an Aristocrat

Diana Frances Spencer was born on July 1, 1961, at Park House near Sandringham, Norfolk, in England. Her parents, John and Frances Spencer, were known as the **Viscount** and **Viscountess** Althorp, or British nobility from the Althorp region. Diana had two older sisters, Sarah and Jane, and soon her younger brother, named Charles, would join the family as well. Like all of us, Diana's story started before her birth, at the time of her parents' marriage.

# Noble Lineage

**Peerage** is the complex legal system of titles that structures traditional English nobility. These titles are made from three separate parts: division, ranking, and type.

Division refers to the region of the United Kingdom where the title originated, such as Ireland or England.

Ranks are what we most commonly think of as titles. There are male and female variations, which are stated before the person's name. These are the five English ranks by order of importance: Duke/Duchess, Marquess/Marchioness, Earl/Countess, Viscount/Viscountess, and Baron/Baroness. Often, a lower title is bestowed on the children of ranked nobility. For example, an Earl's son may be known as a viscount for much of his life, until he takes on his father's title. Diana's father did just that and would later be known as the eighth Earl of Spencer.

Lastly, there are different types of peers. Life peers are those who have been newly appointed within their lifetime to their title, and whose children cannot take on their title. There are representative peers, who are ranked in order to participate in the House of Lords, the upper house of the parliament of the United Kingdom. The most traditional type of peer is the **hereditary peer**, or someone who received their titles from their family.

These titles, along with inheritance, have been traditionally passed down from one male family member to another, as part of a patriarchal system. A **patriarchy** is a legal system where only men may hold power, claim inheritance, or otherwise enjoy legal rights. When the UK was ruled by the **monarchy**, or ruled by the Royal Family, the law strictly enforced these systems. Today, however, titles only exist to serve as signs of respect, courtesy, and tradition.

## The Social Event of 1954

On June 1, 1954, Frances Ruth Roche married Edward John "Johnnie" Spencer at Westminster Abbey. Frances was shy and, at age eighteen, the youngest woman to be married at the church in five decades. John, however, was thirty years old, with a wealth of adult experience. He had fought in World War II and had even served as an aide to the governor of South Australia. Despite their age differences, the couple looked picture-perfect together. John was a tall and dashing gentleman, while Frances was an image of youth and beauty.

The wedding was known as the social event of the year. Queen Elizabeth, her husband Prince Philip, sister Princess Margaret, and Elizabeth and Margaret's mother, the Queen Mother, were in attendance. The royal family had even lent the couple St. James's Palace for the reception. This was because, in addition to being part of British nobility, both the bride and groom had more direct ties to the monarchy. Frances's mother, Baroness Fermoy, had served as the **lady-in-waiting**, or assistant, to the Queen Mother for over thirty years. Her father, Baron Fermoy, had gone hunting with King George VI the day before he died. John, too, had a connection to the crown. He worked as an **equerry**, or an attendant with military experience, to Queen Elizabeth II during her commonwealth tour after the death of King George VI.

After the wedding, the family moved to their first home, Park House, on the grounds of the queen's own

Diana's parents on their wedding day at Westminster Abbey on June 1, 1954

Sandringham Estate. The following year, the new Viscountess Althorp gave birth to their first daughter, Sarah. Two years later they had a second girl, Jane. While both parents loved their daughters, Frances felt the pressure to have a son so that the Althorp title and estate could be passed on. In 1960, she gave birth to John Spencer. Their joy was short lived, however, as he died within eleven hours. The death of their first son would put a considerable strain on the couple and add to the eventual deterioration of their marriage. One year after John's death, Diana was born. After three daughters, in 1964, Frances finally gave birth to the couple's only son, Charles.

## The Early Years

Life at Park House started out happy enough. Originally a guesthouse for the queen, the estate housed ten bedrooms and four salons, and had plenty of gardens and greenery for the children to play in. This space was home to some of the Spencer family's warmest moments. Mary Clarke, Diana's childhood nanny, described life during this time as "wonderful, free, and easy." Robert Spencer, Diana's cousin, described the siblings as "full of fun," and that Diana herself was a "happy little girl." Because her sisters were further apart in age from her and Charles, Diana looked after Charles in a sort of motherly way. Mary Clarke said that this was typical for Diana, who was a girl who loved to be helpful and to have fun:

*Diana mostly enjoyed going to the beach. When we'd [arrive] at the beach hut, Diana would be rushing around, setting everything up, getting the water on so we could all have a drink. [The children] would have competitions to see who could jump from the top to the furthest down. Some of them used to roll the whole way down. They would wander around collecting shells. It was a very carefree time.*

## Divorce, Titles, and Second Marriages

However, the family's picturesque life soon came to an end. In April 1969, Diana's parents formally separated. Divorce was uncommon during that time, especially for well-to-do families. Even more unusual was that Diana's father won custody of the children: at the time, default custody was normally awarded to the mother. The family was scrutinized socially for their unusual and unhappy personal life, adding to the overall stress that comes with divorce. Going forward, Diana and her siblings would be shuffled between their estranged parents' homes.

Many people think that Diana suffered from depression and bouts of mental instability, and suggest that these illnesses started at the time of her parents' divorce. However, others say that this was not that case. Diana knew little about the sordid details of her parents' divorce and regularly saw both parents. Those close to her said she dealt with the divorce as well as could be expected, while others think it was the starting point for troubles later to come.

In June 1975, when she was fourteen, Diana's grandfather died of pneumonia. His passing would provoke many changes for the family. First, they moved from their home at Park House to the ancestral estate of Althorp in Northamptonshire, England. This was a huge adjustment: Park House was a cozy and inviting home for the Spencer children, unlike Althorp, which seemed a large, barren, and even spooky manor. At first this move was difficult, but eventually the Althorp estate became home.

The second big change caused by their grandfather's death was the change in titles for all members of the family. Diana's father, John Spencer, was no longer the Viscount of Althorp but had become the eighth Earl Spencer. Her brother Charles was now the new Viscount of Althorp, while Diana and her sisters received their very first title of "Lady." Teacher Penny Walker said Diana could not contain her excitement: "She rushed along the corridor with her dressing gown billowing out behind her saying, 'I'm a lady, I'm Lady Diana!'"

Almost one year later, in July 1976, Diana's father remarried to Raine, Countess of Dartmouth. The Spencer children were very upset about their father's decision to remarry. They taunted the Countess relentlessly, and Diana's sister, Jane, refused to speak to her stepmother for two years. Even though Diana was very devoted to her father, she did not welcome the addition of the Countess to the family either. Her cousin Robert felt that Diana's feelings weren't against Raine in particular, but that she wouldn't have been happy about any woman who took her father's attention away from his family.

## A Picture of Youth

As a young girl, Diana was very enthusiastic, but she was also shy. Mary Clarke said Diana loved to eat, so

Diana as a young, active child

she would often go into the kitchen and "chatter away
to the staff [and then] cajole them into giving her this
and giving her that." She became very extroverted when

comfortable among friends and family and enjoyed showing off the skills she excelled at, such as music and dance. Two of her favorite activities were swimming and diving. According to her nanny, she would often "run to the top of the slide and stand there poised, as she was beautiful and slim, and shout to everyone 'Look at me! Look at me!'" Penny Walker, Diana's childhood music teacher, said the young lady was very popular at school and was part of a group of girls who were "headstrong and lively."

Diana, however, was not academically inclined. First attending a local school called Riddlesworth Hall, Diana was eventually moved to a boarding school at West Heath School. There she struggled with her schoolwork, trying hard to overcome her difficulty with learning, but with little results. Diana failed all of her "O" exams, a series of pass-or-fail tests given in the UK in order to earn a General Education Certificate (GCE) at the "ordinary" level. This was essentially the equivalent of a high-school diploma in the United States. Penny Walker felt that a lot of Diana's academic problems stemmed from problems at home with her family. She lost concentration easily, and her mind always seemed to be somewhere else.

## A Talent for Compassion

While Diana was not particularly book smart, she did possess terrific people skills. Diana would ride her bicycle to visit older ladies and do their shopping for them. Penny Walker saw that she had "real talent for dealing with people," and that she enjoyed engaging with others. "That was quite unusual," Penny Walker said, "for people of that age."

Diana also helped run dances at the Darenth Park Hospital for the Mentally Ill and Physically Handicapped. Muriel Stevens, hospital manager at the time, found Diana's personality and approach to working with patients exceptional:

*Diana was actually very relaxed, which was quite amazing because it was intimidating and overwhelming to walk into that huge place, with the level of noise, and to see some of the very severely handicapped people ... She had most definitely a natural talent for communicating with very vulnerable people ...*

*I remember seeing Diana do something that I was quite amazed [by]. She appreciated that when people in wheelchairs were taken onto the dance floor, because the handles are behind them, they were being whizzed around but they weren't actually dancing in the same way as other people. Diana danced backwards and drew the wheelchair towards her by holding the arms of the wheelchair. Now that actually is incredibly agile and clever.*

## Pin-Up Prince

To Diana and her school friends, Prince Charles was a heartthrob. She kept photos of him and idolized him as if he were a teen celebrity, musician, or actor. He was considered England's most eligible bachelor: handsome, wealthy, and athletic, he made girls' hearts race. The British media dubbed him "Action Man" because of his interest in challenging and dangerous sports. The *Toronto Star* listed his many interests:

*He was known for steeplechasing, polo, scuba diving, parachuting, piloting helicopters, skiing, sailing and windsurfing back when that sport was new. He was known as a skilled fox-hunter and angler who fished for salmon each summer in frigid, fast-flowing rivers.*

He had served in the Royal Navy and Royal Air Force and had traveled the world giving speeches, and he was well educated. **Paparazzi** snapped photos of him alongside models, daughters of diplomats, and some of the world's most beautiful women. All of England was captured by his charm and intrigued by his romantic interests.

What made Prince Charles's image even more tantalizing was his proximity; since Diana and her schoolmates were upper-crust nobility, they had the promise of actually interacting with the prince and the

Prince Charles in his polo outfit—the epitome of "Action Man"

royal family. Diana would realize her dreams of dating the handsome prince.

## Meeting the Prince for the First (Real) Time

As a child, Diana was a playmate to Prince Charles's younger siblings, Prince Edward and Prince Andrew. This is how Charles thought of her when they were reintroduced to one another in 1977. Diana's older sister, Sarah, was dating Prince Charles at the time and brought the two together. A family friend described the meeting:

> [Diana] taught him how to tap-dance on the terrace. He thought she was adorable ... full of vitality (liveliness) and terribly sweet. [He was struck by] what a very amusing and jolly and attractive sixteen-year-old she was.

Diana would later gush about it to all her school friends. She thought that Prince Charles was "amazing," but while the prince enjoyed her company, he felt Diana was too young to consider romantically. It would be another three years before the two reconnected in a more meaningful way. Sarah and Charles would date for a little longer, but eventually the romance fizzled much like the prince's many previous flings.

## Finishing School

In 1977, Diana left the Heath School to attend a finishing school called Institut Alpin Videmanette in

Rougemont, Switzerland. A finishing school is a school that teaches young women skills they might need in upper-class society. This includes the ability to entertain guests, the use of polite manners and proper etiquette, and other types of social graces. Today, there are very few finishing schools left, due to the changed role of women within the family. However, at that time, for women who lived high-profile lifestyles, these schools existed to teach students how to navigate the tricky and particular rules of nobility. While at the institute, Diana studied life skills like cooking, foreign languages, and sports. She still disliked school and struggled academically. It didn't help that she was only one of nine English-speaking girls at the school or that all classes were conducted in French. After her first term, Diana asked her father if she could leave. With his approval, she left Switzerland and returned to England to look for work.

## CHAPTER TWO

# A Young Woman in London

In 1978, at the age of seventeen, Diana took a job as a nanny for Major Jeremy Whitaker and his wife Philippa at their country home, the Land of Nod estate, in Headley Down, Hampshire. Diana's close friend, William Van Straubenzee, who was Philippa's brother, introduced her to the Whitakers. At the Whitaker's estate, Diana was enlisted to care for the couple's two-year-old daughter, Alexandra, for three months. Even though Diana was a noble Lady, she worked and was compensated like any other nanny: her wage was sixteen pounds a week for typical caregiving tasks like laundry, child-rearing, and tending to domestic affairs.

Diana, working as a nanny, walks with her American ward, Patrick Robertson.

## Life in London

When her job at the Whitaker home ended, Diana moved to London. At first, she lived in her mother's apartment while Frances was away in Scotland, where her mother stayed for most of the year. However, when Diana turned eighteen, she received the birthday gift of her own apartment. The flat, located in the fashionable district of South Kensington at Coleherne Court in Earls Court, cost £100,000. She shared the apartment with three roommates: Carolyn Bartholomew, Anne Bolton, and Virginia Pitman. Later, Diana would recall this as one of the happiest times of her life:

> It was nice being in a flat with the girls. I loved that—it was great. I laughed my head off there. I loved being on my own.

She would live there with her three roommates until 1981.

Initially, Diana worked odd jobs, such as cleaning her sister Sarah's apartment and teaching youth dance classes. However, both these jobs ended after Diana was involved in a skiing accident that took her three months to recover from. Perhaps the injury was a blessing in disguise, because when she returned to full health, she was more determined to find meaningful work.

## Kindergarten Assistant and Nanny

In fall of 1979, Diana took on two part-time jobs
working with children. The first was as an assistant
teacher at the Young England Kindergarten in Pimlico.
The kindergarten was situated in a modest church hall
but welcomed the children of some of England's most
elite delegates, nobles, and entrepreneurs. Kay Seth-
Smith, an older graduate of Diana's alma mater, West
Heath, ran the preschool. While she knew Diana had not
had formal training with children, she felt she had other
qualities to offer:

> *She did have a natural way with children. She was very
> good about getting down to their level, both physically and
> mentally. She didn't mind at all sitting on the floor, having
> children climb all over her, and she talked to them … at eye
> level.*

Diana was always eager to help prepare lunches for
the children and to do other domestic chores that needed
to be done around the nursery. Diana fit perfectly in
the kindergarten and both the children and adults were
appreciative of her generous nature.

Six months later, Diana took on an additional job
as a part-time nanny at the Occasional and Permanent
Nannies Agency in Beauchamp Place. She signed a
contract with the agency under the following terms:

she would work two days a week, never on weekends or weeknights, and within only the most central and well-to-do neighborhoods of Sloan and Belgrave Squares. It was through this agency that Diana began working with an American family, the Robertsons.

## The Robertsons

In May 1979, the Robertsons had their first child, Patrick, in New York City. Pat Robertson worked for Exxon while Mary Robertson worked as a bank officer for Morgan Bank. In January 1980, Mr. Robertson was asked to take a temporary assignment in London. At first, Mary was dismayed, feeling she would have to endure a long-distance arrangement so early in their son's life. However, after approaching her personnel department, they offered her a six-month leave of absence from her position and a part-time job in the London office. Mary felt this was extremely generous, especially for the finance industry, which was not very accommodating to women at the time. Her new position in London would be to train workers at the Saudi International Bank, which was partially owned by Morgan Bank, on American credit standards and procedures. Mary was eager to begin, but needed to find a nanny for the two days she would be working.

Mary called the Occasional and Permanent Nannies Agency, which sent Diana over right away. Mary recalls her first impressions of Lady Diana:

> *She stood calmly, her head slightly bowed, looking up at me through her bangs. She was lovely, with perfect English skin, a slight blush on her cheeks, and clear blue eyes. She simply glowed with youth and good health … At the time, I did not realize that her upper-class accent and flawless manners meant this was no ordinary babysitter. Nor did I realize how young she was because she was so poised and graceful. I simply thought, "Thank heavens. Here's someone I could leave Patrick with."*

The two sat in their living room and discussed the duties she would have in the home. All the while, Diana ruffled Patrick's hair affectionately, gave him toys, or hugged him. Mary would always remember how warm and spontaneous Diana's interaction with her son had been. She felt there was an instant connection between Patrick and Diana. Mary then asked Diana why she had wanted to take on another job, in addition to working at the kindergarten. Diana simply said, "I adore working with children." Mary hired Diana on the spot, without even checking her references. Lady Diana started working for the Robertsons on February 14th, Valentine's Day.

## Courting the Prince

Meanwhile, the busy young Prince of Wales, between his girlfriends, sporting adventures, and diplomatic

engagements, casually announced that he would marry
by the age of thirty. However, by 1980, Charles was
thirty-one, going on thirty-two, with no indication of a
serious paramour. In the absence of any leads, the British
press began to excitedly theorize about who might be the
future Princess of Wales.

Charles was preoccupied with other things besides
his relationship status. Despite being called the "Action
Man," a term he never liked, Charles could be very
introverted, and he prized his privacy and intellectual
pursuits. Like most people who live their lives in the

When not in the spotlight, Charles was a reserved and studious man.

public eye, Charles had to find a way to balance an energetic public persona with a more reserved internal personality. He found reading, hunting, and private trips to the country to be a source of relaxation. Likewise, he cherished his personal relationships with friends and family.

That is why, when his beloved uncle and godfather Lord Mountbatten died, the prince was brokenhearted. Charles's own grandfather had died when he was very young, so he often looked to Mountbatten for paternal advice and guidance. When an Irish Republican Army (IRA) bomb killed

Mountbatten in 1979, Charles was devastated. He had lost an important family member, but even more than this, he had lost the comfort of a man who understood the challenges of royal life and emotionally supported

Lord Mountbatten, a respected statesman and Naval officer, was Charles's most beloved confidant.

him. He continued to attend social events, but those who knew him personally could see he was disheartened.

Diana, too, was attending events and balls. Because she had kept her nights and weekends free of work, she could mingle with British nobility in a way she never had before. She was entering the world of society as a young, attractive woman, and society was responding in kind. Diana attracted many romantic admirers due to her charming manners, beautiful dancing, and elegant fashion. However, Diana wasn't interested in meaningless sweet talk and often spoke to her friends about how she hoped to find her true love. It would be at one of these society parties that she would reacquaint herself with Prince Charles, her first crush.

## Fateful Barbecue

In July 1980, Diana's friend Philip de Pass invited her to a party at his weekend home in the country. The two friends attended a polo match together to watch Prince Charles play. Later, Philip hosted a barbecue for the polo

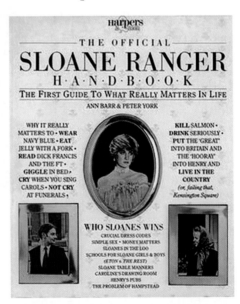

*The Official Sloane Ranger Handbook,* part fashion document and part parody, featured Diana on the cover.

## Sloane Rangers

In 1982, Ann Barr and Peter York, along with the editorial team at *Harpers & Queen* magazine, published *The Official Sloane Ranger Handbook*. This tongue-in-cheek book was intended to explore the habits of young, upper-class English women known as "Sloane Rangers" or "Sloanes." The term first appeared in 1975 in *Harpers & Queen* to describe a newly emerging fashion and cultural archetype. The name comes from Sloane Square, a well-to-do neighborhood located in Chelsea, and the television character the Lone Ranger, to describe the group's fondness for equestrian hobbies and the fashionable way they wore silk neck scarves. Sloane Rangers prized traditionalism and "what really matters": one's background, tradition, the aristocracy, the English countryside, jobs in London, the army, and the status quo. The *Handbook* sums up this sentiment by stating, "the Good Stuff is here already and always has been." Sloanes tended to be outdoorsy and love sports, dogs, and "fine old things." Their fashion reflected traditional English culture, including chic riding gear, hunting outfits, sweaters, collared shirts, and other styles Americans would call "preppy." Sloane Rangers believed in a specific trajectory for the proper woman: grow up in the country, attend a respected university or finishing school, hold a job and live with roommates in the city (for a time), socialize, get married, and return to the country. Diana, in her days before becoming a princess, embodied this type of person. Today, the term has expanded to include men and women and is a beloved fashion subculture.

team and his friends. At this barbecue, Diana had her first chance to make a real impression on the Prince of Wales.

During the party, Charles and Diana stepped away from the activities and found somewhere private to sit. They began to chat. Most earnestly, Diana said to the prince:

> *You looked so sad when you walked down the aisle at Mountbatten's funeral. It was the most tragic thing I've ever seen. My heart bled for you when I watched. I thought, "It's wrong, you're lonely, you should be with somebody to look after you."*

Charles was taken aback. Most people who spoke to him were either too polite or too afraid to bring up sensitive topics with him. Here was a woman who was genuinely interested in his feelings and didn't shy away from sad topics. The two spent most of the evening lost in conversation. Charles even invited Diana to return with him to Buckingham Palace the next morning, but Diana declined because she felt it would be rude to leave her host Philip. Neither one was too concerned, though—it was obvious that they would see each other again very soon.

## Romancing the Throne

A few weeks after the party, Charles invited Diana to go with him to see a performance of Verdi's symphony *Requiem* at the London Royal Albert Hall. Diana brought along her grandmother, Lady Ruth Fermoy, to serve as the couple's chaperone. After the concert, the three returned to Buckingham Palace for a late dinner. This was the first of many invitations Diana would receive. Soon, she would be a guest on the royal yacht, *Britannia*, during a series of races called Cowes Week. After this, Diana was invited to a royal summer estate, Balmoral, in Scotland.

This invitation was more a serious gesture than the previous ones. Most of Prince Charles's companions had never been invited to the Balmoral estate. For Diana, this was an exciting, but nerve-racking prospect: she would be staying with the prince and the royal family for an extended weekend. This was the first quality time Diana would have with the queen, and she would need to present herself as suitable company.

Diana was aware that one needed to be composed and discreet when interacting with the royal family, partly due to her older sister Sarah's experience dating Prince Charles. In an interview with *Time* magazine, Sarah told reporters, "I'm not in love with him. And I wouldn't marry anyone I didn't love whether he were the dustman or the King of England." It was unclear whether these feelings were genuine or just a way of playing "hard to get," but either way, Prince Charles ended the relationship and the queen shunned Sarah.

With this in mind, Diana consulted her sister Jane, whose husband was a member of the royal staff, on proper etiquette. She hoped to learn any information that might help her make a good impression, or at least avoid an embarrassing misstep. In the end, her preparations worked wonders—the royal family was won over by Diana's friendly, considerate, and charming manners. She was invited back to Balmoral for a second time.

## The Press in Pursuit

It was on this trip that Diana received her first taste of the British media. Charles and Diana were fishing by the banks of the River Dee when they spotted binoculars in the bushes across the river. A reporter and two photographers were waiting for them, hoping to catch a glimpse of the prince's next paramour. Diana, however, had a few tricks up her sleeve. Ken Lennox, a photographer for the *Daily Star* who tried to sneak a picture of Charles and Diana that day, remembered the scene:

> I jumped out of the car [but] the girl disappeared into the trees behind Prince Charles. He continued to fish as if there was no one was with him. I watched for ages and then I saw a hand coming around a tree with a compact mirror She pushed it 'round and wiggled it a bit to see where we were, then walked away in a straight line, keeping the tree between us and her. I thought, "My God, who is this he's got here? This is interesting."

While Ken and his colleagues were unable to snap a photo of Diana's face, her identity would soon be discovered. This was the start of the British press's unrelenting obsession with Diana.

When Diana returned home, she knew things had changed. Reporters waited outside her apartment, hoping to catch a shot of her as she went about her daily business. One newspaper photographer rented the apartment across from her own to get a better look into her bedroom. She was bombarded by phone calls at all hours of the night. The paparazzi even followed her to work.

The press had begun waiting outside the Young England Kindergarten and so, in an effort to appease them, Diana and her boss Kay Seth-Smith agreed to let them photograph her with a few children. The photograph showed a beautiful, compassionate, and friendly young girl. However, it also showed off more than Diana had hoped: she had worn a thin skirt and, photographed with the light behind her, the silhouette of her legs showed clearly through the fabric. Kay Seth-Smith said that when Diana saw the photograph reproduced in the papers she "took one look at it, went bright red, and put her hands up to her face in absolute horror." Charles, however, took the photograph with good humor and reportedly said, "I knew your legs were good, but I didn't realize they were spectacular."

This infamous photo, meant to highlight Diana's gentle nature, instead showed off her long legs.

By 1981, Diana was photographed constantly at work
and during her weekend trips with Charles. Evidence
of the time they spent together only proved what the
Spencer family and the royal family already sensed:
the inevitable engagement of Lady Diana Spencer and
Prince Charles of Wales.

# CHAPTER THREE

# *Becoming a Princess*

I n February 1981, Charles returned to England from a trip to the Alps and told Diana he needed to speak to her about something important. He invited her to stay the weekend at Windsor Castle. During that weekend, on February 6, Charles sat beside Diana and asked if she would be his bride. Overwhelmed and embarrassed, Diana's first reaction was to giggle. Charles explained to her how serious this proposal was: she would not only be his wife, but could someday become the queen of England. He also warned her that being in the royal family meant an extreme amount of pressure.

Charles and Diana pose for photos during the public announcement of their engagement.

Charles offered her time to think about it, but Diana excitedly agreed without another moment's hesitation.

## Announcing to the World

On February 24 at 11 a.m., Buckingham Palace's Press Office released a brief statement:

> *The Queen and the Duke of Edinburgh are pleased to announce the engagement of His Royal Highness, the Prince of Wales, to the Lady Diana Spencer, daughter of Earl Spencer and the Honorable Mrs. Shand-Kydd.*

The couple looked dashing together. The media was especially captivated by Diana's engagement ring. Created by jeweler Garrad, the ring was worth £28,000 at the time it was made. The design featured a brilliant, blue, twelve-karat Ceylon sapphire from Sri Lanka, surrounded by fourteen diamonds, and set in eighteen-karat white gold. The ring matched the color of Diana's eyes and complimented her elegant appearance.

A few hours later, Charles and Diana gave their first television interview as a couple. Charles told BBC reporters, "I'm delighted and frankly amazed that Diana is prepared to take me on." When asked how Diana would deal with the huge change of transitioning from a nineteen-year-old nanny to the Princess of Wales, Diana answered, "With Prince Charles beside me, I cannot go wrong." Other pleasantries and anecdotes were shared, leading up to the big question when reporters asked, "Are you in love?" Diana coyly smirked and said, "Of course!" Charles followed by softly saying, "Whatever in love means." At the time, this was a harmless comment that the press did not focus on. However, history would look back on this as the first shred of evidence that perhaps the couple viewed their marriage with different eyes.

## Goodbye to Single Life

Only a few months earlier, in December 1980, Diana's job with the Robertsons had ended when the family returned to New York. As a going-away present, Diana gave them a dark green, leatherbound photo album with "1980" stamped in gold, to hold all the memories of their time together in London. With heartfelt hugs and wishes, the family departed, telling Diana, "we care very much for you and will help you in any way we can, whatever happens." Later, Diana would go on record to say the year spent with the Robertsons and young Patrick was, "the happiest year of my life."

Diana was now facing a whirlwind of change. A few days after the televised announcement, she moved from her flat at Coleherne Court into Buckingham Palace. She said goodbye to her roommates and left her job at the kindergarten. Diana was to spend the next six months transforming herself into the future Princess of Wales.

## Training to be a Princess

Diana arrived at the palace as a shy, nineteen-year-old girl. In fact, during her engagement, the media would dub her "Shy Di" because of the way she often ducked her head and gazed away from the camera. Diana desperately needed to find her confidence and stride. However, unlike most women, Diana would be maturing under the inquisitive eyes of the British media, the royal family, and the entire world.

There was at least one thing Diana was not concerned about: she was Anglican, not Catholic, a religious requirement for royal family members. However, it would take a lot more than that to become a princess. Diana began "training" as soon as she was moved into her spacious new rooms in Buckingham Palace. A biography of Diana's life describes the nature of this "schooling":

*She spent her days learning royal protocol—how to talk to the public, how to shake hands, how to treat the household servants, even how to wave to the crowd.*

There were many royal rules to be followed: one must wear hats and bright colors in public in order to stand out from the crowd, wave from the elbow and not the wrist, and never use a public bathroom. Later, Diana would be quoted saying, "The worst thing about being a princess is having to pee."

Furthermore, she would be required to participate in many cultural, traditional, and charitable events. The palace courtiers explained to Diana that her royal engagements would average about 170 a year. This would include attending horse races, like the Ascot Races in the Berkshires; tennis championships, like Wimbledon; military ceremonies, such as "Trooping the Colors;" the ceremonial opening of Parliament; the Chelsea Flower Show; hospital benefits; and various other charitable events.

To round out all the etiquette and practical knowledge, Diana was also required to read up on royal family history. She studied stacks of historical records and volumes of books in order to learn about English legacy and nobility.

Often, Diana went to the Clarence House to "study" under the **tutelage**, or instruction, of the Queen Mother, Charles's grandmother. Here, the Queen Mother further guided the young fiancée on proper royal behavior. This training was especially valuable because the Queen Mother had also been a **royal consort**, or spouse of the ruling monarch, to the former king of England, George VI. As an outsider to the royal family, the Queen Mother had sympathy for Diana and tried to help her prepare for her new role.

## Diana Takes a Plunge

Despite this careful training, Diana encountered many difficulties on the road to becoming royalty. The first challenge came on March 9, 1981, only a few weeks after their engagement. Charles and Diana were making their very first public appearance as a couple at a gala at Goldsmith's Hall. The event raised funds for the Royal Opera House in London and was strictly a "black tie affair," meaning male guests had to wear black ties and other formal attire.

Diana wanted to follow suit and wore a stunning black gown for the occasion. Later she would recall, "Black to me was the smartest color you could possible have at the age of nineteen. It was a real grown-up dress." The dress, however, proved to be more scandalous than she had hoped.

First, unbeknownst to Diana, wearing black was a breach of royal protocol. For centuries, black outfits had been reserved for funerals only. Some accounts say that Prince Charles explained this to her before leaving for the gala. Others say that she was unaware, but would later learn of her mistake from the angry Queen Elizabeth.

Even more scandalous than the color was the cut of her dress. Diana had picked the dress "**off-the-peg**," also known as "off-the-rack" in America, from the then largely unknown English designers David and Elizabeth Emanuel. This meant the dress was ready-made and not specifically tailored to properher own measurements. The strapless taffeta dress that Diana had chosen featured a low-cut neckline that showed off too much of her body.

Diana in her scandalous black dress at the Royal Opera House Gala

BBC reporters recalled hearing gasps as Diana stepped out of the car.

For any other woman, this dress would have been perfectly acceptable. However, because the future Princess of Wales wore it, the media went wild. Flurries of photographs were taken, which would be published the next day alongside newspaper headlines. The *Daily Mirror* wrote, "Lady Di Takes the Plunge," the *Sun* exclaimed, "Di the Daring," the *Daily Express* remarked, "Shy Di Shocks," and even the *Times* commented, "Shy Di R.I.P." The press had up to this point regarded Diana as a baby-faced Sloane Ranger, innocent and reserved. This was the first indication that she perhaps had a more daring side.

## Problems Ensue

Diana did not anticipate the reaction her outfit, or her body, would cause. The media focused on her every curve, noting that she had a "blooming physique" and "bounteous figure." Most comments were complimentary, although they had a negative effect on Diana's already distressed mind. Her first foray into the public eye as the prince's fiancée had backfired and Diana felt she had failed both in her social graces and in her appearance.

### Eating Disorder

Diana was more stressed than she had ever been before. Due in part to the pressure from the media, she refused to eat but would then give into cravings for sweets. This was the beginning of a long battle with bulimia, which would last eleven years. **Bulimia nervosa** is a serious eating disorder characterized by binge eating followed by purging in order to avoid weight gain. Bulimia is a disease that affects the body and mind: sufferers experience anxiety, guilt, and shame regarding their attitudes toward food and their own body. Diana's older sister, Jane, had also suffered from an eating disorder in her early twenties. During this time, Diana could not yet see the connection between her sister's illness and her own, nor was she able to fully understand the relationship between physical health and mental health.

## Loneliness

In addition to her own personal issues, Diana struggled with her new relationship with her husband-to-be and his family. She longed to spend time with her new fiancé, but as a prince, he was often employed in other duties. During their six-month engagement, Charles made a five-week tour of the United States, Australia, and New Zealand, and Diana missed him terribly.

She also found Buckingham Palace to be very lonely. Large, formal, and quiet, the palace was a starkly different environment than that of her former London apartment. She did not realize how separate the family lived: physically distanced by the size of the palace, unable to spend time with one another because of royal obligations, and emotionally estranged because of tradition and formality. She would later recall her longing and loneliness during this time:

*I missed my [roommates] so much I wanted to go back there and sit and giggle and borrow clothes and chat about silly things, just being in my safe shell again ... I couldn't believe how cold everyone was [at Buckingham Palace].*

## Camilla Parker Bowles

Diana was especially distressed by the presence of one of Prince Charles's ex-girlfriends, Camilla Parker Bowles. Charles and Camilla had begun dating in 1971. Then, in 1973, Charles was called overseas to join the Royal Navy, and the relationship ended abruptly. Many people have speculated on why the two parted ways—some say Charles wasn't ready for a serious relationship, others say that Camilla was interested in someone else, and yet others say that Lord Mountbatten persuaded Charles otherwise. Regardless of the specific reason, the royal family did not consider Camilla a suitable match because she lacked noble **pedigree**, or ancestral heritage. So, in July 1973, when Camilla married Royal Lieutenant Andrew Parker Bowles in what was the society wedding of the year, no one thought twice about her former relationship with the Prince.

However, Charles and Camilla's relationship was anything but behind them. The two stayed very close friends, and Charles relied heavily on her for emotional support. When engaged to Diana, Charles received regular phone calls from Camilla, which he always took in private. Camilla and her husband were frequent weekend guests at the royal country home, Sandringham. When Diana would start to feel unsure or jealous about this relationship, she would ask Charles to assure her that they were only friends. He responded by telling her that it was all in the past and that his days of romance with Camilla were over.

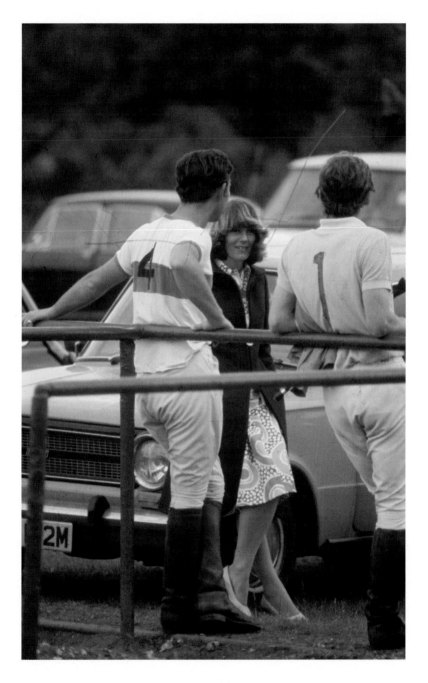

A young Charles and Camilla Parker Bowles at a polo match

In the weeks before the royal wedding, Diana noticed a strange package tucked among the various wedding gifts. Michael Colborne, Charles's personal aide and friend, tried to stop Diana from opening it, but to no avail. What she found inside was a gold bracelet with a lapis pendant engraved with the initials "F" and "G." Diana was furious; she knew the gift was for Camilla because the two called each other by the pet names "Fred" and "Gladys." She was also angry because Michael refused to answer any questions about the present, other than he had ordered it at the request of the prince.

Diana confronted Charles, who admitted he had ordered the bracelet as a farewell gift to Camilla, signifying the end of their relationship. Diana, in tears, found this explanation hard to believe. Just four days before her wedding, she would be in tears again, but this time she was caught on camera. Diana attended a polo match Charles was competing in. Still unsettled and distraught by this recent argument, Diana broke down in tears and had to be escorted away from the prying eyes of the press.

## Luncheon of Doubt

On Monday, July 28, just one day before the wedding, Diana had lunch with her sisters Sarah and Jane. She spoke candidly with them about her fears over Camilla and debated if she should call the wedding off. Her sister Sarah said, "It's bad luck, Duch," using the family

Decorative plates were just one of many kinds of royal wedding souvenirs made.

nickname for Diana, "your face is on the tea towels, so you're too late to chicken out now." She was right—there was no turning back.

## Wedding of the Century

Finally, the big day, July 19, 1981, had arrived. To mark the occasion, the United Kingdom declared it a national holiday. The queen had sent more than 2,500 invitations to friends, family, heads of state, and the crowned royalty of Europe. The Robertsons, Diana's former employers, were among the few, if not the only, non-elite guests to be invited to the affair. More than 600,000 people gathered in the streets, and the ceremony would be televised to over 750 million people worldwide.

When Diana awoke, she could hear people cheering and singing. Her rooms in Buckingham Palace faced out toward a road called The Mall, which was filled with

## Royal Wedding Souvenirs

In the months preceding Charles and Diana's wedding, shops across England were stuffed with commemorative souvenirs: tea towels, mugs, tins, and even Rubik's cubes decorated with the English flag or the happy couple's portrait. This was by no means a new phenomenon. The tradition can be traced back to 1840 with the wedding of Queen Victoria and Prince Albert. After the industrial revolution, mass manufacturing was in full swing, and excitement for the royal wedding led to the production of mugs, plates, and jugs. These mementos served as a piece of history that could be owned, and while only the wealthy purchased these expensive items, the precedent and fervor for favors was set.

Princess Elizabeth II and Prince Philip's wedding was held on November 20, 1947, and occurred during **British austerity**, a five-year stretch after World War II marked by reduced public expenditures. Since there were very few industrial supplies, and most people did not have disposable income, only a few wedding souvenirs were produced. This is just one of the reasons why the next royal wedding, that of Charles and Diana, was so lavishly celebrated by the English people.

The most recent royal wedding of Prince William to Catherine Middleton has carried on the tradition. Their wedding souvenirs ranged from elegant to kitschy and even tongue-in-cheek, and reflected more modern tastes and sensibilities.

attendees. In these rooms, she prepared herself to be the next Princess of Wales.

The same designers who had created her controversial black gown, the relatively unknown designers David and Elizabeth Emanuel, also created her wedding dress. It was elaborately constructed from ivory silk taffeta, hand embroidery, sequins, and about ten thousand pearls. The most striking feature was the twenty-five-foot train made of silk and antique lace that trailed behind her. To literally top it off, Diana wore the Spencer family tiara and a bridal veil. Charles dressed in a ceremonial naval officer's uniform.

To accommodate the large crowd, the wedding took place at St. Paul's Cathedral, rather than the traditional Westminster Abbey. St. Paul's could hold more people and created a longer route for Diana's procession, allowing more spectators to catch a glimpse of the bride. Starting at the Queen Mother's home, Clarence House, Diana and her father rode in a horse-drawn stagecoach to the church.

But the carriage was too small to fit Diana, her father, and her twenty-five-foot-long dress. So when she stepped out of the carriage and onto the red carpet, her dress was wrinkled. Her bridesmaids frantically worked to shake out the imperfections, but in true Diana fashion, she kindly whispered to them, "Just do your best."

Diana's father proudly took his daughter's arm and they proceeded to the altar. The feeling of romance in the air was **palpable**, or so intense that it could be felt physically. Diana would later recall her memories of the occasion:

> *I remember being so in love with my husband that I couldn't take my eyes off him. I absolutely thought I was the luckiest girl in the world. He was going to look after me.*

During the exchange of vows, Diana accidently said, "Philip Charles Arthur George" instead of the correct "Charles Philip Arthur George." Charles, too, made an error saying he would offer her "thy goods" instead of "my worldly goods." The couple had also agreed before that Diana would not promise to "obey" Charles as is customary in traditional vows.

The crowd cheered ecstatically—Diana had finally become the Princess of Wales. The married couple walked down the aisle, back into the stagecoach, and proceeded to a breakfast reception for 120 guests at Buckingham Palace.

Upon arrival at the palace, five-year-old bridesmaid Clementine Hambro, the granddaughter of Winston Churchill and the Princess's favorite kindergarten student, tripped and fell. Diana bent down in her full bridal regalia to comfort the crying girl, gently asking her, "Did you bump your bottom?" This kind gesture once again showed the British public their new princess's humility and compassion.

Charles and Diana leave the cathedral after their royal wedding.

Once Clementine's tears were dried, Diana, Charles, the royal family, and members of the wedding party appeared on the palace balcony to greet the masses. They waved to an excited crowd, which in return cheered for the newlyweds. Happily, the couple kissed, providing the perfect ending to an already perfect fairytale wedding.

## CHAPTER FOUR

# Remaking Royal

A shower of rose petals met the newlyweds as they departed the palace for their honeymoon. They boarded a private train that took them to the Broadlands for a few days in the country. Immediately after, the new husband and wife embarked on a two-week Mediterranean cruise on the royal yacht *Britannia*.

## Honeymoon

Diana had been eagerly awaiting her honeymoon. For the first time since their engagement, she would be able spend quality time alone with Charles. However, things

Charles and Diana during one of their first interviews as a married couple did not go as she had hoped. The couple was required to attend formal dinners, parades, and other engagements, which kept the two from sharing more private moments. In addition, Diana and Charles had different personal interests. The biographer Joanne Mattern described the state of the trip:

At the Broadlands, Charles was more interested in fishing than talking to Diana. Even worse, Charles brought a set of philosophical books along. He expected Diana to read the books and then discuss them with him at dinner. For Diana, who hated academics and wasn't interested in philosophy, this was a crushing disappointment. Instead of getting to know her husband, Diana spent much of the time sleeping or visiting the servants' quarters, where she enjoyed sharing bowls of ice cream and talking to the staff. It was hardly the romantic honeymoon with her Prince Charming that she had imagined.

The couple also had their first real argument on this trip. One evening, Charles put on a pair of cufflinks given to him as a gift by Camilla. Diana protested, but he wore them all the same.

After the cruise, the couple spent a month at the royal estate of Balmoral in Scotland. Once again, Charles spent hours outdoor fishing, hiking, or riding horses, while Diana was left to entertain herself. Friends of Charles and the royal family came to visit them at Balmoral, but most of them were older than Diana and she had little in common with them. Between her royal obligations and encounters with the press, she had little time to communicate with friends from her former life. Diana had hoped this would change after the wedding, or that she would at least spend more time with her new husband, but her isolation at Balmoral made it clear that this would not be the case. Instead, Diana spent her days feeling bored and lonely. When she asked Charles if she could return to London, he refused, saying the royal family always stayed for a month and she would just have to get used to it. One palace courtier described the prince's state of mind:

*Lovely chap though he was, Charles gave no indication of thinking through what getting married to him would be like for Diana. He carried on with his merry ways, his extracurricular bachelor life. To her, it was a massively bigger thing.*

Unfortunately, their life together would not be the happy union that Diana had expected.

## The First Walkabout

Three months after her wedding, Diana would have her first **walkabout**, a public event where members of the royal family greet and speak with bystanders in the crowd. The couple headed to Wales where, after two intense days on tour, they arrived at the tiny town of Brecon.

During the event, Charles and Diana each walked along one side of the street greeting people from the crowd. Then they switched sides to allow everyone to have the chance to meet both of them. The Mayor of Brecon, Gwanwyn Evans, recalled that, "every time this happened you had this huge [disappointed], 'Awww,' from the people that [Diana] was leaving." Bystanders would call "Di, Di, Di!" to beckon her over to their side of the street. Mayor Evans also remembered how friendly and approachable Diana was:

> She was so conscious of the small children behind the barriers and, [regardless] of the fact that that outfit of hers must have cost a mint, down she [went], not just bending, but ... on her haunches to these little ones behind the barriers.

Up to this point, Charles had always been the center of attention. One courtier recalled the prince glumly kicking a pebble and saying, "They don't want to see me." Later that evening at a gala, Diana expressed her gratitude in the region's native tongue of Welsh, after which Charles gave a speech. He tried to make light of his bruised ego:

> *I've come to the conclusion that really it would have been far easier to have had two wives, to have covered both sides of the street, and I could have walked down the middle directing the operation.*

The couple continued to tour, with each new audience reacting in the same way. Photographer Ken Lennox remembered the public's growing interest in the princess:

> *In the midst of all this walkabout and touring, Diana wouldn't do anything. Charles would do lots of things: he would make speeches, a lot of the speeches he felt were quite important because he'd have a huge audience ... He'd work hard at the speech and ... the next day nothing would appear of Charles ... It wasn't the "Charles and Diana show," it was the "Diana and Diana show."*

Diana's popularity continued to surge, precisely because she was so different from other royals. In addition to her beautiful looks and fresh energy, she appeared genuinely interested in people. During walkabouts, Diana had no qualms about crossing barriers to speak to and touch ordinary individuals. Even the

During royal walkabouts, Diana loved to engage with the crowd, especially children.

media praised Diana: the *Sun* newspaper dubbed her the "Queen of Hearts" for the way she enthralled audiences. Just by being herself, open and friendly, Diana had become a princess of the people.

## Darling of the Press

Before Diana was married, she approached Ronald Allison, Buckingham Palace Press Secretary, to ask if the media madness would end after the wedding. He told her the truth: it would never go away.

British newspapers employ a different type of journalism than their American counterparts. Ron Smith, the author of *Ethics in Journalism*, notes that Americans are often "shocked" when they first read British newspapers. Reputable papers will often use outrageous headlines and photos, something more akin to trashy newspapers or tabloids in the United States. However, newspaper consumption in the UK is much higher than in the United States: Smith notes that, in 2011, the *Sun's* circulation was nearly twice that of *USA Today* or the *Wall Street Journal*, despite serving a much smaller population. According to Smith, when competition for readership is high, moral standards are low:

*The British tabloids have long been locked into heated circulation wars, and often they veer from what would be called the standards of responsible journalism.*

Diana was experiencing this lack of "responsible journalism" firsthand. She was the target of tabloids and paparazzi as she went about her daily life. By the end of her life, Diana would be the most-photographed woman in the world. For a woman who was barely twenty years old, this was too much attention to handle.

In November 1981, a crowd of photographers cornered Princess Diana leaving a sweet shop. Enough was enough: in an unprecedented move, the queen

## The British Press, or Fleet Street

"Fleet Street" is a **metonym** to represent the British Press. The English printing and publishing industry was first established on Fleet Street in central London during the early 1500s. Early printers made the written word readily available to the masses and thrived on printing everything from legal documents to books and plays. It wasn't until March 11, 1702, that the first English newspaper appeared. The *Daily Courant*, located on Fleet Street, was printed, published, and written by Elizabeth Mallet. Fearing the stigma, mockery, and censorship that would have come from being a female publisher, Mallet stamped each newspaper with the gender-neutral phrase "sold by E. Mallet." The single-sheet paper published articles on news abroad and prided itself on unbiased reporting, stating there was no need for editorial comments when "people had sense enough to make reflections for themselves."

By the twentieth century, Fleet Street was home to the country's most well-known papers and tabloids, including the *Times*, the *Sun*, the *Daily Express*, and the *Daily Telegraph*. The majority of English households bought a paper from one of these publishers working on Fleet Street. However, in 1986, the *Sun* and the *Times* were relocated to Wapping, East London. Since then, many other publications have moved out and been replaced by banking and financial institutions. Fleet Street is still home to a handful of publishers and its many pubs and bars continue to cater to a journalistic crowd. It also has a place in pop culture: Fleet Street is a square on the English version of the board game Monopoly.

stepped in to help. Less than a month later, she asked
for a meeting with all the top editors from British
newspapers, tabloids, magazines, and television stations.
Queen Elizabeth reprimanded the "Fleet Street"
reporters for their constant harassment, which, she said,
placed the princess under "great strain." The palace
press secretary added that the princess felt "totally
beleaguered," and this treatment would no longer be
tolerated. The queen would eventually sue the *Sun*
for slander and stop them from publishing a series of
scandalous stories about the royal family. For now, the
Queen had temporarily halted the barrage of reporters
circling around Diana.

## Heir to the Throne

Soon, Diana was eager to step into her next big role:
motherhood. She had always loved children and had
wanted a family for as long as she could remember. Mary
Robertson, her former employee, recalls the young Diana
saying that she wanted to have at least twelve children.
For the time being, she needed to focus on having just
one child—preferably a boy who could inherit the
British throne.

### First Pregnancy

On November 5, 1981, Buckingham Palace announced
that Diana was pregnant. It had only been about one
hundred days since they were married—no other royal

couple had procreated so quickly—and the media welcomed this exciting, and somewhat unexpected, news. The queen asked reporters to leave the princess alone after the announcement, so much of Diana's first pregnancy was unusually calm and absent of encounters with the media.

Despite the temporary reprieve from the press, Diana still had a difficult pregnancy. She was often struck with morning sickness but still kept up with her royal appearances. In February 1982, it was revealed that Princess Di had fallen down a flight of stairs at some point the month before. Buckingham Palace spokesmen and doctors reassured the public that no harm had been done to either Diana or her unborn child. In fact, after two hours of rest, she was able to accompany Charles to a barbecue.

Diana then caused another stir in the royal family. She wanted to give birth in a hospital and in a more active manner. Traditionally, royal babies had been born at home and mothers were not allowed to decide where or how the delivery would occur. In addition, fathers were not often allowed to help, or even be present, for the birth of their children. Diana had a different vision for her child's birth and, like many of her decisions, this vision influenced other families and medical professionals to rethink birthing traditions.

## Prince William

Toward the end of her pregnancy, Diana was induced early and spent sixteen hours in labor. With Charles by her side, she gave birth to a son. William Arthur Philip Louis arrived on June 21, 1982, at St. Mary's Hospital in London. Everyone celebrated the birth of the new heir to the royal throne. The following morning, Charles cheerfully greeted the press by saying William was "in excellent form, thank goodness—and looking a bit more

Charles and Diana with their first-born son, William, at his christening

human this morning." After showing off the newborn baby on the hospital steps, the couple headed to the newly-renovated Kensington Palace in London.

The following months were very happy. Charles and Diana eagerly accepted their new roles as father and mother. Each had grown up with parents who were either distant or absent, and both wanted to raise their child in a close-knit and loving household. The couple made very few public appearances the first two months after William was born. Unlike most royalty, Diana wanted to be a part of her son's life as much as possible. It was reported that she was the first royal mother to breastfeed. She took care of young William like any loving mother would: she changed his diapers, fed him, and bathed him. When William was ten weeks old, the couple hired a nanny to help, but as biographer Joanne Mattern states, "Diana made it clear that she expected to be the baby's main caregiver."

## Australia and New Zealand Tour

In March 1983, Charles and Diana were scheduled to leave for a six-week tour to Australia and New Zealand. Prince William was only nine months old, but tradition mandated that children stay behind. Prince Charles recalled his own childhood was marked by loneliness when his parents left for months at a time on goodwill tours. He did not want this for his son. Diana, too, could not imagine leaving her son for so long. She asked the queen for permission to bring William along with them and, surprisingly, the queen allowed it. Prince William became the first royal baby to go on a foreign tour. The decision to include her son, author Daisy Goodwin notes, made the princess even more popular: "No woman wants to leave her baby, and that was what made Diana so lovable—that she always absolutely adored her children."

The tour was a huge success, and thousands came out to see the royal couple. Crowds cheered Diana's name, brought her bouquets of flowers, and screamed when they caught a glimpse of her driving by in an open-top car. At the time, Charles was proud his wife was causing such a stir. But Lord Palumbo, Charles's good friend and polo teammate, recalled how Diana's public perception would change the couple's relationship:

*She did take center stage. This was one of the problems that came between her and the Prince of Wales—that she ... became such a glamorous figure as his wife that she stole the limelight. I don't think he minded that initially ... in fact I think he was rather pleased and proud. But it grew irksome as the time went on.*

## A Mother of Two

In early 1984, Diana became pregnant with her second child. This time, she experienced less severe morning sickness. In anticipation of the birth, Charles even decided to cut back on public engagements to spend more time with the family. Diana would later remark that the six weeks leading up to her second son's birth were the happiest time of her entire marriage.

## It's a Boy

As her date approached, only one thing worried Diana. Charles had repeatedly said he wanted a daughter; in fact, he seemed to expect it. Diana had seen her ultrasound and knew that she was going to have a boy. She decided to keep this news a secret from her husband.

On September 15, 1984, Diana returned to St. Mary's Hospital in London and delivered her second son, Henry Charles Albert David, or Harry, as he would be known. Diana had again opted for an active birth and, once again, Charles had stayed by her side the entire time. However, this time, Charles made a few thoughtless comments that turned the joyous occasion sour. Joanne Mattern describes:

*Charles was clearly disappointed, and the first words out of his mouth were, "Oh God, it's a boy." Charles also commented negatively about the baby's red hair, which was a common Spencer trait.*

As the couple left the hospital, it seemed all of England had come to greet them. Champagne corks popped, church bells rang, and two traditional forty-one-gun salutes rang through the air. Charles shook hands, accepted a baby pacifier as a gift, and even jokingly had to persuade a young lady from giving him a congratulatory kiss, saying, "I've had enough excitement for one day."

However, Diana was distraught and angry. As Charles put on a good show for onlookers, Diana knew there was trouble brewing in their marriage. She would remember thinking:

*Then suddenly as Harry was born it just went bang, our marriage, and the whole thing went down the drain ... something inside me closed off.*

William, Diana, and Harry enjoyed a ski trip in Lech, Austria.

The birth of a child should be a joyous occasion for a family. Unfortunately, the additional stress of another newborn would cause additional rifts in Charles and Diana's already crumbling marriage.

## Rebel Royal Mum

Diana is remembered for many things, but she wanted to be most remembered for being a loving mother. She got her wish: today, Diana is still admired for the way she humanized the royal approach toward raising a family. Rob Wallace of ABC News notes how Diana "paved the way for a new kind of royal parenting, setting a standard for mothering a future monarch." By rejecting the "arms-length" method, Diana created a deep bond with her children. Judy Wade, royal contributor to *Hello!* magazine, recalls that, according to sources within Kensington Palace, "Every morning the boys would run in their pajamas into her bedroom, and she'd have her arms open wide to hug them." This love fueled and inspired Diana, who admitted, "I live for my sons. I would be lost without them."

To keep her children happy and healthy, Diana felt it was important to raise them with as much "normalcy" as possible. Patrick Jepson, Princess Diana's chief of staff, noted how the simple things made all the difference:

*She made sure that they experienced things like going to the cinema, queuing up to buy a McDonalds, going to amusement parks, those sorts of things that were experiences that they could share with their friends.*

This often meant breaking with royal traditions in favor of a more hands-on approach. William was the first royal family member to attend public school. Diana's sons saw life outside the palace walls and created friendships with all types of people, not just nobility. Judy Wade would dub her the "rebel royal mum" for the many breaches in protocol she made for the sake of her children. As an adult, Prince William would describe his mother's efforts:

*She played a huge part in my life and Harry's growing up, in how we saw things and how we experienced things … She very much wanted to get us to see the rawness of real life. And I can't thank her enough for that, 'cause reality bites in a big way, and it was one of the biggest lessons I learned is, just how lucky and privileged so many of us are—particularly myself.*

Diana wanted to instill her children with a sense of honor in their royal station and urged them to treat people with care and consideration. Diana took her sons to homeless shelters and hospitals for charitable work. Ken Wharfe, William's personal bodyguard, recalls one particular trip when Diana took her seven-year-old son to a homeless shelter:

> This was done completely out of sight of any camera or media. This was Diana's way of actually saying to William, "Listen, it isn't all what you think it is living at Kensington Palace." That was a quite a brave thing on Diana's part.

Patrick Jepson, Diana's aide, respected Diana for her "clever" approach to raising two children who would have "distinctive [and] unique" lives of obligation. He remembers her priming William from a young age to handle the media, which he always despised. William's first public outing was at age ten. Jepson watched as Diana prepared her son:

> Diana said to William, "It only may be ten seconds out of your life, [but] it could be years of happy memories for the person you meet." That sense of respect for people in the crowd is something that I think we can see Diana has passed on very successfully to her children.

In many ways, Diana came into her own because she had realized her dream of being a parent. When she first arrived at Buckingham Palace, she was shy and compliant, but in the course of having two children, Diana transformed into an individualistic and determined mother. Though her marriage had already begun to collapse, she would always be strong and steadfast in her job as a parent. It was this role as nurturer that would lead her toward her life's passion and help her to shape her own identity as a princess.

# CHAPTER FIVE

# *Fashion Icon and Humanitarian*

Since becoming a princess, Diana had tried to reconcile her own desires with those of the British monarchy's. She felt overlooked and dismissed by the royal family. To them, her only role was to be a wife and mother to the future heir. Diana, however, wanted to use her position to make a difference in the world. Lord Palumbo knew of her frustration to find a place among the royal family:

> *The princess of Wales felt she had a contribution to make: that she was talented, that she had a wonderful sense of communication, that it wasn't appreciated as it should have been.*

Diana during a 1983 tour of Australia

As her marriage became more of a disappointment to Diana, she focused outward, on her public life. She began to assert her independence in the only way she knew how—through her public image—and started to help herself by helping others.

## Fashion

Wardrobe and appearances have always been quintessential to royal life. For centuries, monarchs have posed for portraits in their finest garb, creating visual testaments to their wealth, status, and power. These paintings and photographs captured sitters wearing gorgeous **couture**, or fashionable made-to-measure clothes, decorated with the finest jewelry and accessories money could buy. However, as Colin McDowell, author of *Diana Style*, aptly states, "What nobility tend to possess is not fashion sense, but style."

Royal style, as McDowell describes it, meant adhering to well-made outfits that flattered the individual but did not necessary adapt to changes in fashion. At best, this creates a timeless look, but, at worst, it constructs an image of someone stuck in the past. If fashion dares to reinvent bodies and images, then traditional style aims to keep looks stable and unchanging.

Fashion has bigger implications than just a shirt or a pair of shoes: it is one of the most visible ways people express their identity and values. So as Diana redefined royal style, she also redefined the way people think about the British monarchy and women in power.

## Building a Wardrobe

On the day of her engagement, Diana said she owned "one long dress, one silk shirt, and one smart pair of shoes." In fact, most of the outfits she was photographed in belonged to the photography studios. In many ways, royal fashion was more about theatricality than style. The queen herself referred to her official clothes as "props," and as McDowell notes, "all royal designers [had] to be aware of the need to balance couture and costume." Diana's wedding dress was the perfect example of this: it had been designed with a public and TV audience in mind, and she wore it as an actress would wear a costume.

Once officially a princess, Diana's wardrobe would need to accommodate her various official duties. Most events called for formal dresses or suits, all of which had to be made by British designers. Diana also needed clothes for many different occasions and had to avoid repeating outfits as much as possible. On some days, Diana even changed her clothes four times. Another royal tradition required that she wear hats and gloves for almost all her public appearances, accessories that are hard to match.

At first, it was difficult to balance strict protocol and personal taste. Diana's early wardrobe, as described by *Vogue*, was often, "too fussy, too startling in its primary colors, and too middle-aged with its pussycat bows and feathered hats."

However, Diana would soon transition from dress-up doll to statement maker with the help of *Vogue's* fashion editor, Anna Harvey. The two would become close friends and work together to find Diana's unique style. Harvey noted the challenge with Diana would be to find the "middle way between the pie-crust collared blouse and the catwalk," meaning the balance between respectability and fashion-forward thinking.

## A Fashion Sense of One's Own

Diana soon found she had a natural instinct to use her clothes as a form of communication. In November 1982, she attended a charity event wearing a dropped-waist, one-shoulder, blue silk dress that was reminiscent of designs worn in the thirties. She accessorized the dress with a pearl choker. As McDowell describes, this fashionable outfit was a change in mindset:

> *The dress was a departure for a royal princess—it would be difficult to imagine [another princess] being comfortable in such an outfit at an official function—and showed that Diana was not afraid to innovate.*

When Diana was pregnant, she helped change the way designers thought about maternity wear. At the time, most designers tried to create outfits that concealed a mother's baby bump. Diana, however, was extremely proud of her form. She challenged her designers to create feminine and flattering dresses that showcased her pride. Where pregnancy had once been seen as unsightly, Diana made it visible and stylish.

## Diana's Effect

Diana's fashion decisions had an immediate impact in the fashion world. Designer Roland Klein remembers:

*She was very influential. She put fashion and London designers in the front of the public at large. When she was wearing something that was photographed, it had an immediate effect.*

Designers saw huge boosts in sales after Diana modeled their creations. Department stores would be flooded with orders for knock-off items similar to outfits the Princess had worn. It was reported that Diana's love of high heels enabled a factory in Northern Ireland to stay open because of the thousands of orders she inspired. She has been credited with invigorating the entire British **millinery**, or ladies' hatmaking, industry. The "Diana effect" did not just influence commoners—even the queen adopted shoulder pads in 1986.

## Dancing with the Stars

Diana's position as a fashion icon was in full swing in more ways than one. In November 1985, the royal family took a goodwill tour to the United States.

John Travolta and Diana dance at the White House in 1985.

In Washington, DC, they attended a White House reception for President Ronald Reagan. Diana chose a navy blue column dress designed by Victor Edelstein. The dress's bare shoulders and bustle were inspired by paintings of Edwardian dinner outfits and invoked a timeless elegance.

The queen had given Diana a sapphire brooch to wear with the dress, but she disliked the stuffiness and weight of it. Instead, Diana hooked the brooch onto a choker necklace, and the effect was beyond chic. Wearing her elegant outfit, she spun on the dance floor to "You're the One That I Want" with movie star John Travolta. The pair, both excellent dancers, stole the show. It was said that Prince Charles was upset by what he considered a flashy performance, but Diana didn't care—for the first time she was enjoying being glamorous and fun.

This phase of Diana's fashion would be known as the "Hollywood Years," and it peaked in the late eighties. The last of her "fairytale" dresses debuted in 1988 on a trip to Paris. This gown, her most expensive at an estimated £55,000 (almost $100,000), was a formal dinner dress in an oyster-colored satin with a long-sleeved bolero jacket. The jacket was a hit with the media: it recalled the regal splendor of princesses past, but with a modern twist.

## A New Identity

In the early 1990s, Diana shed her former sweetheart identity for a new, powerful, adventurous, and serious persona. Since 1981, her main designer had been Catherine Walker. Entirely self-taught, Walker took up patternmaking as a means to support her children after the sudden death of her husband. Diana and Catherine found they had a lot in common and became good friends. So, when the princess decided to change her wardrobe, she reached out to Catherine for help.

The friends decided that Diana's change in mind could be shown visually through emphasizing her

Early in her fashion career, Diana would wear frillier dresses and hats, eventually abandoning them for a sleeker, more contemporary look.

broad shoulders and natural height, which reflected an air of confidence and control. Diana abandoned the frilly clothes of her past and embraced straighter skirts, shoulder pads, and sharper silhouettes. McDowell remarks that the fashion of the time enabled a woman to be "very feminine and yet 'masculine' and strong." Diana now appeared as a professional working woman with the style to match.

Diana also worked with hair stylist Sam McKnight, who "changed the princess's hair almost instantly, making it shorter and yet more relaxed." This would be one of Diana's most iconic looks. Even critics could now see the change, remarking that her new hairdo showed off her newfound confidence.

## Outfits that Mean Something

When touring internationally, Diana wanted her outfits to comply with local etiquette and culture. In Muslim countries, she wore more modest clothes, covering her head with silk scarves when visiting mosques. On trips to India, she wore dresses with intricate beadwork and patterning, reminiscent of designs found on the borders of Indian paintings. For a trip to Dubai, she wore a pink, red, and gold outfit made from vegetable dyes, a nod to traditional Bedouin colors. Her fashion choices were also made for more practical reasons: once, on a trip to Brazil, Diana was advised not to wear the soccer team's colors of green and yellow because they had recently lost to Argentina. She was also told to avoid wearing blue and white, the colors of the Argentinian team, or a riot would ensue.

## Princess Di Is Wearing a New Dress

In 1986, the English band Depeche Mode released an album called *Black Celebration*. One of the most influential records of the 1980s, it was immediately praised for its uniquely dark sound and lyrics. So when it was revealed that the track "New Dress" was about Princess Diana, it may have seemed out of place. However, the song is one of the band's most overtly political and poignant tunes.

"New Dress" starts aggressively—a stomping beat and bass line are accompanied by electronic shots, as if from a laser gun. The lyrics are plucked straight from the grisly headlines of British tabloids: "bomb blast victim fights for life," or, "famine horror, millions die." By hearing these headlines out of context, the song highlights the media's obsession with violence.

In the song, the British press is also obsessed with something else: "Princess Di is wearing a new dress." This line alternates with lyrics of increasing violence, pointing out how the media is more concerned with frivolities, like fashion, than serious world problems.

Then a more upbeat chorus chimes in:

"You can't change the world/But you can change the facts./And when you change the facts,/You change points of view./If you change points of view,/You may change a vote./And when you change a vote, You may change the world."

The message is ultimately positive: though the media may focus on superficial things, someone like Diana can make a difference because she changes the way people think, even when doing something as simple as wearing a new dress.

Diana was also considerate enough to dress appropriately for charity work. When visiting sick children, she would wear bright colors to cheer them up. She even dubbed one dress by David Sassoon, a silk piece with brightly colored abstract flowers in turquoise, yellow, and red, as her "caring dress." If she were visiting the blind, she would wear clothes with interesting textures so they could feel her presence. For children, she wore dangling necklaces, careful that her jewelry and buttons were free of sharp edges. She would forego the royal etiquette of wearing gloves so she could intimately meet with people. Diana defended her approach by saying, "Yes, I do touch. I believe that everyone needs to be touched."

## Activism

Starting in the mid-1980s, Diana would find her life's passion in charity work. As Princess of Wales, she had always been expected to make appearances at schools, hospitals, and charities. However, she soon discovered that she had an interest in helping above and beyond her royal obligations.

### HIV/AIDS

In the 1980s the world was gripped with fear over the AIDS epidemic. **HIV**, or Human Immunodeficiency Virus, is a disease that attacks the body's immune system and its ability to fight off other diseases. The later stage of

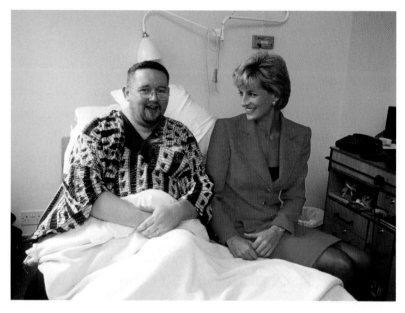

Diana loved to be close to the people she served: here she visits with a patient at a London Lighthouse center for AIDS.

HIV infection is known as **AIDS**, or Acquired Immune Deficiency Syndrome, and is marked by a rapid decline of a patient's health, which increases the likelihood of pneumonia, extreme weight loss, skin lesions, and cancers. There is no cure for AIDS, but today there exist medications that can slow the disease's progress and prevent secondary infections.

In the 1980s, however, this was not yet the case. At the time, not much was known about the disease, like where it had come from, how it was spread, or why it was so aggressive. Before 1996, patients with AIDS were given an eighteen-month life expectancy. In the UK, scare headlines implied people could get HIV by kissing, touching, and even more farfetched theories like sharing the communal wine at church.

On April 9, 1987, Diana was invited to open a new AIDS wing at Middlesex Hospital, the first of its kind in the country. Dr. Michael Adler, chairman of the National AIDS Trust, asked if she would shake hands with patients to show the disease was not contagious through touch. Diana's personal staff advised her to wear rubber gloves, but the princess refused. One of the most iconic photographs of Diana's career would capture the compassionate moment when Diana shook hands with these AIDS patients. This simple but meaningful gesture impacted the way the world viewed the disease. Dr. Adler later remarked, "It made a tremendous impact—just a member of the royal family touching someone. It was a colossal impact."

Diana helped to **destigmatize** the perception the public had of those living with the disease. She said, "HIV does not make people dangerous to know. You can shake their hands and give them a hug. Heaven knows they need it. What's more, you can share their homes, their workplaces, and their playgrounds and toys."

Throughout her lifetime, Diana would visit and support hundreds of hospitals, centers, and charity events for adults and children living with AIDS and HIV. In 1991, she became the patron of the National AIDS Trust, or NAT. That same year she went back to Middlesex Hospital with First Lady Barbara Bush on a highly publicized visit. Diana supported NAT, even after leaving the royal family, until her death in 1997.

Diana was especially sensitive to children living with AIDS. In 1989, while visiting a hospital in Harlem in New York City, Diana was seen hugging a small boy with AIDS. The *Los Angeles Times* wrote,

> *For two or three minutes, the worlds of poverty and plenty were united as the princess and the patient stood in the hallway, the little boy's head on Diana's shoulder, his arms around her neck.*

In 1990, Diana opened "Grandma's House," a home for HIV-positive children in Washington, DC, and in 1991, she visited a shelter in São Paulo, Brazil, for abandoned children living with AIDS.

In March 1997, she met with Nelson Mandela to discuss the growing AIDS epidemic. While Diana would not live to see the fruit of her efforts in South Africa, their plans were realized in November 2002, when the Nelson Mandela Children's fund and the Diana, Princess of Wales Memorial Fund announced they were launching a new program to combat AIDS. This effort would aim to improve the lives of more than six hundred thousand families and orphans affected by HIV. Nelson Mandela, one of history's greatest activists for human rights, thought highly of the princess's efforts:

*[Diana had used her celebrity status to] fight stigma attached to people living with HIV/AIDS ... She transformed public attitudes and improved the life chances of such people ... Her love for children went beyond the European borders and boundaries.*

## Leprosy

Less well known was Diana's support of leprosy patients. **Leprosy** is a disease that causes extreme skin and nerve damage and, though it is not very contagious, it can be transmitted through contaminated respiratory fluids. For centuries, leprosy was deemed incurable and "lepers" were sent to live in isolated colonies, cut off from society. Today, leprosy is curable, but many of the world's poorest areas are still affected and unable to afford cures.

In 1989, during an official visit to Indonesia with Prince Charles, Diana asked to visit the Sitanela Leprosy Hospital to meet with patients. Upon her return to the UK, she became a patron of the Leprosy Mission in Britain and continued to support them until her death. Diana would say, "It has always been my concern to touch people with leprosy, trying to show in a simple action that they are not reviled, nor are we repulsed."

Diana would continue to visit hospitals and projects in India, Nepal, Nigeria, and Zimbabwe. **Posthumously**, the Diana Princess of Wales Health

Education and Media Centre was opened near New Delhi in India. Established in 1999 with a grant from the Diana, Princess of Wales Memorial Fund, the center's purpose was to "promote the rights, dignity and inclusion of people affected by leprosy and disability into Indian society."

## Homelessness

In 1989, Diana made her first high-profile solo trip overseas to New York City. While there, she visited the Henry Street Refuge for the Homeless on the Lower East Side. The refuge was accustomed to visiting celebrities who, as director of the center Verona

Middleton-Jeter would say, were "on a guilt trip ... [and] not really concerned about our people." However, when Diana arrived she proved that her motivations were different.

When she arrived, Diana immediately started chatting with the directors and volunteers, even making the joke that she and the director were "wearing the same

Diana visiting the Day Center for Young Homeless in 1990

colors," as both were in pink outfits. One administrator dropped a button and Diana handed it to her saying, "We have to keep up with these little things!" The staff was immediately won over.

Diana then headed to the shelter to speak with a young boy in his bedroom. They chatted about his Michael Jordan poster, and she helped him tie his shoe. Staff member Frances Drayton remembers Diana fondly:

*The questions she asked, the way she had asked them, her concern about not even asking questions until the press left, was all out of respect for who we were ... Everything was genuine and she fit right in ... She was happy to be here, you could tell. Such a beautiful person ... She's still here, a piece of her, she left that here.*

Diana's efforts deeply impacted many, including her son William. In 1992, Diana became the patron for Centrepoint, a charity that provides accommodation and support to the homeless. It was one of the charity's homeless shelters that Diana took William to as a boy. William was so affected by this experience that Centrepoint was the first charity he became a patron of, and he has supported them ever since.

## Landmines

Diana was also the patron of HALO, a nonprofit organization that cleans up the debris left from war, specifically landmines. She was concerned about how these devices caused serious injuries, often to children, even years after a conflict has ended.

In January 1997, Diana was photographed in khakis, a helmet, and a **flak jacket** while touring a minefield in Angola. The publicity from these iconic images helped bring attention to the issue, and in June of that year, Diana spoke at a landmines conference at the Royal Geographical Society in London. She then went on to Washington, DC, to promote the American Red Cross's landmine campaigns. Just days before her death, Diana went to Bosnia and Herzegovina with members of the Landmine Survivors network to visit landmine removal projects.

Her efforts helped passed the Ottawa Treaty, which banned the use of **antipersonnel** landmines, or landmines intended to kill people. This international bill, signed after Diana's death, was made official by the United Nations in 1997. The campaign even received a Nobel Peace Prize. Foreign Secretary Robin Cook paid tribute to Diana when he introduced the bill into the British House of Commons in 1998, by thanking her for the "immense contribution" she had made in making the bill a reality.

## A Life of Charity

Diana supported hundreds of charities and causes in her lifetime. She helped with organizations that supported

Diana in a flak jacket and khakis touring a minefield in Huambo, Angola. This visit and her work for HALO were highly publicized.

cancer, mental illness, and drug abuse, in addition to her work with AIDS patients, and victims of landmines and leprosy. In 1993, Diana spoke out to four hundred experts who had gathered in London to discuss eating disorders—an issue the world would later learn was also close to her heart.

This type of charity work, though fulfilling, was not easy: Diana remain composed while in the public eye, but as soon as she was alone she would break down in tears from mental, emotional, and physical exhaustion. However, Diana did not ever disparage this important work, saying, "I knew what my job was, it was to go out and meet the people and love them." For all the compassion she sent out into the world, it seemed the world loved her back equally.

# CHAPTER SIX

# New Beginnings and Endings

Charles and Diana's marriage had been falling apart since the birth of their second son. With their royal obligations, the prince and princess now rarely saw one another. It was also a well-known "secret" that Charles had been seeing Camilla Parker Bowles for some time. By the early 1990s, both William and Harry were enrolled in boarding school, and Diana only saw them on weekends. Between her charity work and royal obligations, Diana was alone. Lord Palumbo described the discrepancy between her private and public lives:

Despite years of turmoil, the royal family was often pictured as happy while in public.

> *She would go back to Kensington Palace in the evening and have dinner by herself on a tray on her knees watching television ... She found [this] disturbing— the adulation on the one hand and the loneliness on the other.*

When Charles was home, he and Diana frequently fought. One courtier recalled that Diana "wanted him to stay at home with her and the children. There were tantrums and hysterics. She challenged him—it was the first time he had been challenged." After these fights, William, who was very close to his mother, would hand her tissues to wipe her tears. This turmoil raged below the surface while the palace continued to release staged photographs of a happy family.

## The Press Turn on Charles

The media soon caught wind of the royal family's marital issues and began circulating scandalous headlines. Diana was aware of the power of the media and wanted the world to see her as a compassionate and caring person. If the press was going to depict her family as divided, she wanted to be on the favorable side. Even if the royal family dismissed or discouraged her efforts and concerns, the public at large did not. She could wield her popularity to further her own interests and keep her name above any mudslinging.

The British press had long disparaged Prince Charles. He was seen as out of touch with the people and more concerned about things like polo matches or abstract philosophy. His offhand comments incurred ridicule, and even insults. The final blow to his image was on June 3, 1991, when eight-year-old Prince William was struck in the head by a golf club while playing with his friends. He was rushed to the nearest hospital, where Charles and Diana were told he had fractured his skull. The prince needed a routine operation to remove a piece of cracked bone. Diana stayed by her son's side throughout the procedure, but Charles left for a previous engagement at the opera. The surgery went well, and William was soon at home recovering.

While the operation hadn't been serious, the damage to Prince Charles's reputation was. The *Sun* ran the headline, "What Kind of Dad are You?" This was the first of many displays of favoritism toward Diana. Photographers captured images of Diana embracing her children, while almost no images of Charles made it to the public. Both parents loved their children very much, but it was clear who was being painted as the villain and who was the saint. This began a competition for public favor between Charles and Diana that only accelerated the decline of the royal marriage.

## Annus Horribilis

The queen would refer to the year 1992 as annus horribilis, which is Latin for the "horrible year." The first disaster to strike the royal family was the release of Andrew Morton's biography *Diana: Her True Story*. This book detailed the princess's lonely childhood, loveless marriage, battle with bulimia, and state of constant emotional distress from dealing with the royal family and media. The queen was horrified and felt Diana had crossed the line in allowing Morton to interview her for his book. Charles felt betrayed and angry.

A few days later, Diana's father, the eighth Earl of Spencer, passed away. Diana made it very clear that she did not want Charles to be at the funeral, but Charles knew it was royal protocol to make an appearance. The situation was tense, and the public felt he had only shown up for the sake of his public image.

More bad news befell the crown: Prince Andrew and Sarah Ferguson separated, Princess Anne and Mark Phillips divorced, and, in November, Windsor Castle and most of the priceless artworks it housed were destroyed by a devastating fire. The queen asked the public for tax money to pay for the fifty million dollars worth of repairs, but British citizens fiercely protested. The monarchy was on bad terms with the British people.

Then, on December 9, 1992, British Prime Minister John Mayor made an official announcement to the British House of Commons: the prince and princess were separating. This meant that, while they were not legally divorced, they were no longer married either. However, Charles would still one day be king and Diana would someday be queen. Diana found the hardest part of the arrangement was having to arrange time with her sons, and she missed them dearly whenever they were away.

## Finding Herself

For Diana, 1993 was a definitive year. Though she continued to work on behalf of the monarchy, the separation allowed her more freedom to pursue her own agenda. She threw herself into her charity work and mothering. Diana once said, "The biggest disease this day and age is that of people feeling unloved." By loving her children and helping so many vulnerable people, Diana could cure this "disease" for many people—including for herself.

Just as Diana was gaining confidence from her newfound independence, another scandal hit. Photos of her exercising were taken with a hidden camera and published in the tabloid the *Mirror*. This was the last straw—Diana decided she would be effectively retiring from public life. On December 3, 1993, the princess made a speech in which she stated, ""I hope you can find it in your hearts to understand and to give me the time and space that has been lacking in recent years." She withdrew from many of her royal engagements and tried to find some private time to reevaluate her life.

No one could deny that Charles and Diana's marriage was over. On February 28, 1996, at the urging of Queen Elizabeth, Charles and Diana met face-to-face to sign the divorce papers. Diana would share joint custody of the children, retain her home at Kensington Palace, and continued to be called the princess of Wales. Charles did not make any promises, but Diana took his silence as agreement. She announced to the world what had happened, and the furious queen replied that no agreement had been made.

On August 28, 1996, the divorce was finally official. Although Diana would still be known as the princess of Wales, the queen had stripped her of her title "Her Royal Highness," a gesture that was seen by many as mean-spirited. This would have stung

In 1994, the same day a tell-all interview with Charles was broadcast, Diana wore this iconic black dress.

# The Power of the Black Dress

While Diana recovered from the 1993 photo scandal, Charles worked rebuilding his image. On June 29, 1994, journalist Jonathan Dimbleby interviewed the prince of Wales about his married life. As fourteen million British viewers watched, Charles admitted to being involved with another woman who, although not named, was clearly Camilla Parker Bowles.

That very same night, Diana attended a fundraising gala hosted by *Vanity Fair*. She had originally planned on wearing a Valentino dress, but the designer had leaked details to the press against her wishes. Instead, Diana chose a black dress by designer Christina Stramolian. The last time she wore a black dress socially—in 1981, at her first appearance after her engagement to Charles—it had been a disaster. Back then she was shy and unsure. This time, she exuded confidence, strength, and beauty in her short, off-the shoulder cocktail dress. Once again, Diana topped the headlines. The *Mirror* published a photo of her with the caption "Take That!" It was obvious that Diana wouldn't be put down.

Almost one year later, in November 1995, Diana released her counter-interview for a show called *Panorama*. This would be the first time she publicly shared her story in her own words. Diana chose black again: this time, the outfit was a smart blazer, skirt, and pair of sheer stockings. She looked credible and balanced, just like the story she was telling. At least twenty-three million people in England watched the broadcast. Diana said all she wanted was to be "the queen of people's hearts," rather than the queen of England.

more if not for her son, William, who told her, "I don't mind what you are called. You're Mummy."

## Peaceful Beginnings

Author Colin McDowell states that, by this point, Diana had "come into her own as an individual, with strong ideas of how best to salvage her life from the debacle of the royal marriage." The first step would be to cut back on her charity work to focus on those charities most important to her. She received some criticism for this, but pointed out that she was no longer a royal and, thus, could not serve as a "royal" patron. Diana focused on five organizations: the National AIDS Trust, the Leprosy Mission, Centrepoint, the Royal Marsden Cancer Hospital, and the Great Ormond Street Children's Hospital. By allowing herself to focus, Diana also found her next important cause: working to remove landmines.

### Humanitarian

In 1997, Diana took a trip to Angola, Africa, with a BBC crew to photograph and film a documentary about the danger of landmines. Diana made it very clear that she was no longer an envoy of the British monarchy. She would not attend royal dinners or functions, but just learn, observe, and help. For Diana, this was a new way to do charity: on her own terms and completely devoid of protocol.

Diana read statistics and research on the issue, walked through fields that had once been filled with landmines, and even detonated a landmine herself. Mike Whitlam of the Red Cross said, "I can't think of anybody now who could give such a very simple, global message, and get people to listen and take notice."

One person who took notice was Tony Blair, the new Prime Minister of Great Britain. He was impressed with Diana's work and wanted her to take on a new role as

Auction house Christie's sold most of Diana's royal gowns for charity.

Humanitarian Ambassador for Britain. Soon, the Prime Minister and his wife, Cherie, became good friends with Diana.

## Family Healing and The Christie's Auction

After the divorce, relations between Charles and Diana actually improved. Both were devoted parents and found that they could enjoy each other's company because of the mutual love for their children. They attended confirmations, sports games, and trips abroad together as a family. Charles even stopped by Kensington Palace for tea when he was in the neighborhood.

Diana's relationship with her children also had more room to flourish. William was not quite fifteen years old and already one of Diana's most trusted advisors. He was smart, wise, and a polished young man. He understood his mother well and, as Joanne Mattern writes, even came up with one of Diana's most brilliant moves:

> *William knew that Diana was trying to simplify her life and change her image. He suggested that she auction off many of the glamorous dresses she had accumulated over the years and donate the money to charity.*

Diana was floored by this idea and instantly contacted Christie's, a world-renowned auction house in New York. The staff at Christie's agreed that this was a wonderful idea, and the auction was set for later that year.

Diana's auction was one of the greatest social events of the year and helped her raise $3.26 million dollars for charity. Diana's most iconic dresses were sold, including the velvet gown she wore the night she danced with John Travolta, which was auctioned at $222,500. Most importantly, this event was a way of saying goodbye to her former life as a princess. Diana had learned firsthand that privilege is not all it's cracked up to be, and that happiness could be found in living a simpler, more meaningful life. As Colin McDowell puts it: "Diana was increasingly coming to believe that glamour came from within, not from her clothing."

## Final Days and Tragic Death

In 1997, Diana wanted to make her relationship with her new boyfriend, Dr. Hasnat Khan, public. The doctor was reluctant to do so. Frustrated, Diana accepted an invitation from businessman Mohammed Al-Fayed to vacation with him on the tropical island of St. Tropez. Diana brought William and Harry, and together they boarded the private yacht *Jonikal*. This trip was full of good fun and good company. During the vacation, Diana was introduced to Fayed's son, Dodi, and the two hit it off.

A few weeks later, Diana boarded the *Jonikal* with Dodi again. On August 30, they stopped off in Paris. Dodi's driver, Henri Paul, safely drove them to the Ritz Hotel after almost crashing with an aggressive pack of paparazzi that were chasing them. The photographers swarmed outside the hotel, so the couple decided to stay inside for dinner.

Later, Diana and Dodi tried to sneak out the back entrance to avoid the paparazzi. Henri Paul drove and Trevor Rees-Jones, Dodi's bodyguard, joined them. Paul had been drinking and taking medication when he pulled up at 12:20 a.m. to drive the couple away. Immediately, at least six cars and motorcycles began following them. Henri Paul started driving erratically to lose them: he ran red lights at an estimated sixty miles an hour. When they reached the Pont de l'Alma tunnel, which stretched under the Seine River, he brought the vehicle crashing into a column.

Dodi Fayed and Henri Paul died instantly. Trevor Rees-Jones, the only passenger wearing a seatbelt, survived but suffered severe head and facial injuries. Diana was barely alive but unconscious. Eyewitnesses report that the paparazzi began snapping photos of the accident, and the camera flashes flashed in the dark "like machine gun fire."

Diana was treated in the ambulance before arriving at the nearest hospital. While Diana's external injuries were not severe, she was quickly losing blood due to internal damage. While doctors did everything they could to help her, Diana soon went into cardiac arrest and, at 4:00 a.m on August 31, 1997, the beloved princess was declared dead.

## The World Mourned

When Tony Blair heard the sad news he declared, "This is going to produce real public grief on a scale that's hard to imagine." As soon as news of Diana's death spread, people flocked to Kensington Palace to leave flowers, stuffed teddy bears, and lit candles.

When Prince Charles heard the news, he burst into uncontrollable tears. Even though royal family members were only supposed to attend royal funerals, Charles announced he would attend Diana's. The queen objected and, for the first time, Charles pushed back against his mother, saying that the world would be aghast if the royal family did not publicly mourn for Diana. The queen was completely out of touch with how the royal family was perceived: newspaper

Diana's funeral procession in Westminster Abbey

headlines already questioned why the royal family had not returned to London, why the flag was not at half-mast, and if they even cared at all. Eventually, the queen conceded and allowed the family to return to Buckingham Palace, where she would address the nation herself on the loss of Diana.

More than 2.5 billion people watched Diana's funeral procession, a larger audience than the one that had watched Diana's wedding years earlier. Men from both the royal and Spencer families carried her casket and twelve-year-old Harry placed a wreath and a handwritten note for "Mummy" on top of it. Diana was buried at the Althorp estate on an island in the middle of a lake.

## Legacy

It's hard to enumerate Diana's legacy. In the days following her death, musician Sir Elton John re-released his single "Candle in the Wind," and donated the £38 million proceeds to the new Diana, Princess of Wales Memorial Fund. The foundation would award 27 grants to 471 organizations, and spend over £112 million on charitable causes until its closure in 2012.

In 2000, the Princess Diana Memorial Walk, a path that runs through London's parks and includes a playground accessible to handicapped children, was completed. In 2004, the queen officially unveiled the Princess Diana Memorial Fountain in Hyde Park.

Posthumously, Diana received many awards and
accolades for her commitment to charity work.

Most importantly, Diana is remembered for the
many lives she touched, and especially for the influence
she had on her two sons. Both Harry and William have
continued to support charitable works into adulthood.
Before starting college, Harry spent eight weeks in
Lesotho, Africa, working with children orphaned
by AIDS. He stated how his mother influenced his
charitable activities:

*I believe I've got a lot of my mother in me, and I think she'd
want me to do this, me and my brother. I don't want to take
over from her because I never will. I don't think anyone can,
but I want to try to carry it on to make her proud.*

Prince William also honored his mother's memory
by starting a family of his own. In 2011, he married
Catherine Middleton, and the happy family now has two
children, George and Charlotte. By creating a close-knit
family that does not place royal tradition above family
bonding, Prince William can live out another one of
Diana's dreams.

After Diana's death, Nelson Mandela said, "Her
inspiration must continue to change lives." Perhaps
Diana's greatest legacy is that, years after her untimely
death, people are still inspired by her work to make the
world a better place.

## Timeline

**1981**

Charles and Diana's engagement is announced on February 24.

**1967**

Diana's parents divorce

Diana Frances Spencer is born to Frances and Edward John Spencer on July 1.

**1961**

Diana's father marries Raine, the Countess of Dartmouth. That same year, Diana and Charles meet for the first time.

**1977**

Nine-year-old Diana is sent to boarding school.

**1970**

**1984**

On September 15, Diana gives birth to her second son, Prince Harry.

**1982**

Diana gives birth to Prince William on June 21.

**1997**

In January, Diana travels to Angola and begins her campaign against landmines. On June 25, Christie's auction house in New York auctions Diana's gowns; the proceeds are donated to AIDS and cancer research. On September 4, Diana, Dodi Al Fayed, and their driver, Henri Paul, die in a car crash in a Paris tunnel.

Diana and Charles begin a six-week tour of Australia and New Zealand in March.

**1983**

Buckingham Palace announces Diana and Charles's separation on December 9.

**1992**

# SOURCE NOTES

## Chapter One:

Page 6: "Lecture, Tribute to Princess Diana on the Eve of Her Funeral," Buckingham Palace, Westminster, September 9, 1997.

Page 10: "Diana - Princess of Wales Full Biography," YouTube video, 3:12:51, posted by Paulo Carvalho, May 24, 2013, www.youtube.com/watch?v=KE5p2kiZWx8.

Page 12: *Ibid.*

Page 15: *Ibid.*

Page 18: Katz, Gregory, "Prince Charles Seems like the Forgotten Man | Toronto Star," Thestar.com, March 7, 2011. Accessed January 6, 2016, www.thestar.com/news/world/royals/2011/03/07/prince_charles_seems_like_the_forgotten_man.html.

Page 18: "Princess Diana of Wales Biography," www.notablebiographies.com/De-Du/Diana-Princess-of-Wales.html.

## Chapter Two:

Page 22: Mattern, Joanne. *Princess Diana.* (New York, NY: DK Publishing, 2006), pg.11.

Page 23: "Diana - Princess of Wales Full Biography."

Page 25: Robertson, Mary. *The Diana I Knew.* (New York, New York: Cliff Street Books, 1998), Kindle edition.

Page 30: "Diana - Princess of Wales Full Biography."

Page 31: "The Man Who Will Be King," *Time*, May 15, 1978, p. 8.

Page 33: "Diana - Princess of Wales Full Biography."

Page 35: *Ibid.*

## Chapter Three:

Page 38: "Diana - Princess of Wales Full Biography."

Page 39: "1981: Prince Charles and Lady Di to Marry," *BBC News*, February 24, 1981. Accessed January 5, 2016, news.bbc.co.uk/onthisday/hi/dates/stories/february/24/ newsid_2516000/2516759.stm.

Page 39: Robertson, *The Diana I Knew*, Kindle edition.

Page 40: Mattern, *Princess Diana*, pg. 25.

Page 40: Kelley, Kitty. *The Royals.* (New York, NY: Grand Central Pub., 2010), pg. 275.

Page 42: "Diana - Princess of Wales Full Biography."

Page 44: Kelley, *The Royals*, pg. 283.

Page. 45: Waller Rogers, Lisa. "Princess Diana: F & G." Lisa's History Room. July 21, 2010. Accessed January 6, 2016, lisawallerrogers.com/2010/07/21/princess-diana-f-and-g/.

Page 48-49: Mattern, *Princess Diana*, pg. 29.

Page 26: "5 Mini-Disasters at Princess Diana's Wedding," The Royal Fans All About Royal Family, August 11, 2015. Accessed January 6, 2016, www.royal-fans.com/5-mini-disasters-at-princess-dianas-wedding.

Page 52: "5 Mini-Disasters at Princess Diana's Wedding."

Page 52: Hicks, India. "Princess Margaret in Her Nightie, Sweets from the Queen of Tonga and Diana Singing Just One Cornetto! A Royal Bridesmaid's VERY Surprising Big Day," *Mail Online*, January 7, 2011. Accessed January 5, 2016, www.dailymail.co.uk/femail/article-1345229/Royal-wedding-India-Hicks-bridesmaid-memories-Prince-Charles-Dianas-wedding.html.

## Chapter Four:

Page 56: Mattern, *Princess Diana*, pg. 32.

Page 57: "Diana - Princess of Wales Full Biography."

Page 58: *Ibid.*

Page 59: Smith, Ron F. *Ethics in Journalism*. (Malden, Massachusetts: Blackwell Pub., 2008), Kindle edition.

Page 59: "Women's History – Elizabeth Mallet," TYCI RSS, October 14, 2013. Accessed January 6, 2016, www.tyci.org.uk/wordpress/womens-history-elizabeth-mallet.

Page 61: Early, Chas, "June 21, 1982: A Future King Arrives as Princess Diana Gives Birth to Prince William," BT.com, June 21, 2015. Accessed January 6, 2016, home.bt.com/news/world-news/june-21-1982-a-future-king-arrives-as-princess-diana-gives-birth-to-prince-william-11363987656319.

Page 67: Mattern, *Princess Diana*, pg. 40.

Page 67: Wallace, Rob, "Rebel Royal Mum': Diana's Legacy as Parent," ABC News, May 26, 2013. Accessed January 6, 2016, abcnews.go.com/International/rebel-royal-mum-dianas-legacy-parent/story?id=19241646.

Page 68: "Diana - Princess of Wales Full Biography."

Page 69: Mattern, *Princess Diana*, pg. 44.

Page 69: "Hello, Harry!" *People Magazine*, October 1, 1984.

Page 70: Mattern, *Princess Diana*, pg. 44.

Page 71: Wallace, "'Rebel Royal Mum': Diana's Legacy as
   Parent."

Page 72: *Ibid.*

Page 72: *Ibid.*


## Chapter Five:

Page 75: "Diana - Princess of Wales Full Biography."

Page 76: McDowell, Colin. *Diana Style*. (New York, New York:
   St. Martin's Press, 2007), pg. 34.

Page 77: *Ibid*, pg. 69.

Page 78: *Ibid*, pg. 76.

Page 79: *Ibid*, pg. 83.

Page 83: *Ibid*, pg. 103.

Page 84: Depeche Mode. *New Dress*, Black Celebration. Mute,
   1986. Album.

Page 85: McDowell, *Diana Style*, pg. 83.

Page 87: *Ibid*, pg. 127.

Page 88: *Ibid*, pg. 176.

Page 89: *Ibid.*

Page 90: Mattern, *Princess Diana*, pg. 44.

Page 91: *Ibid.*

Page 92: Goldman, John, "7-Year-Old AIDS Patient Shares
   Hug With Princess," *Los Angeles Times*, February 4, 1989.

Page 93: "Mandela and Diana Charities Join Forces," BBC News, November 2, 2002. Accessed January 6, 2016, news. bbc.co.uk/2/hi/uk_news/2392637.stm.

Page 93: "Diana, Princess of Wales," The Leprosy Mission of England and Wales. Accessed January 6, 2016, www. leprosymission.org.uk/about-us-and-leprosy/our-history/ diana-princess-of-wales.aspx.

Page 93: "Humanitarian Work," The Diana, Princess of Wales Memorial Fund. Accessed January 6, 2016, www. dianaprincessofwalesmemorialfund.org/humanitarian-work.


## Chapter Six:

Page 96: "Diana - Princess of Wales Full Biography."

Page 99: Clayton, Tim and Phil Craig. *Diana: Story of a Princess.* (New York, NY: Simon and Schuster, 2013), pg. 125.

Page 101: Mattern, *Princess Diana*, pg. 61.

Page 102: Clayton and Craig, Diana: Story of a Princess, pg. 260.

Page 103: McDowell, *Diana Style*, pg.188.

Page 104: McDowell, *Diana Style*, pg. 189.

Page 105: Mattern, *Princess Diana*, pg. 98.

Page 105: Mattern, *Princess Diana*, pg. 102.

Page 105: *Ibid.*

Page 107: Mattern, *Princess Diana*, pg. 111.

Page 109: "Mandela and Diana Charities Join Forces," *BBC News*, November 2, 2002. Accessed January 6, 2016. news. bbc.co.uk/2/hi/uk_news/2392637.stm.

# GLOSSARY

**AIDS or Acquired Immune Deficiency Syndrome** The final stages of HIV, which is marked by a rapid decline in a patient's health. Symptoms include pneumonia, extreme weight-loss, skin lesions, and cancers.

**antipersonnel** A term for weaponry designed to kill or harm people.

**bulimia nervosa** A serious eating disorder characterized by binge eating and purging in order to avoid weight gain.

**couture** Made to order, tailored, and often specially handmade clothes.

**equerry** A male assistant to the queen with previous military experience. Traditionally the equerry managed the royal stables as well.

**flak jacket** A military-style jacket worn to protect against bullets.

**hereditary peers** Peers who inherit their title through their family.

**HIV or Human Immunodeficiency Virus** A disease that attacks the body's immune system and its ability to fight off other diseases.

**lady-in-waiting** A female assistant to the queen.

**leprosy** A disease that causes extreme skin and nerve damage and is transmitted through respiratory fluids.

**metonym** A name or expression used in place of something derived from an attribute associated with it (e.g. the Crown is used to mean the British monarchy).

**millinery** The trade or business of making women's hats.

**monarchy** Government ruled by a single person, like a king or queen, or a family, in which power is generally inherited.

**off-the-peg** An English term for readymade clothing; the equivalent of the American term "off-the-rack."

**palpable** To feel physically.

**paparazzi** Photographers who make a living by taking photos of celebrities as they go about their daily lives.

**patriarchy** A family, group, social system, or government in which a man or a group of men hold the power.

**pedigree** A person's official, ancestral heritage.

**peerage** The British noble ranking system.

**posthumously** Occurring after someone has died.

**royal consort** The ruling monarch's spouse.

**tutelage** Guidance or instruction.

**viscount/viscountess** A title of British nobility situated below an earl, but above a baron.

**walkabout** A public event where members of the royal family greet and speak with ordinary people in a crowd.

# FURTHER INFORMATION

## Books

Mattern, Joanne. *Princess Diana*. London, UK: DK Publishing, 2006.

McDowell, Colin. *Diana Style*. New York, NY: St. Martin's Press, 2007.

Robertson, Mary. *The Diana I Knew*. New York, NY: Cliff Street Books, 1998.

## Websites

### The British Broadcasting Corporation
www.bbc.com

The British Broadcasting Corporation is the UK's largest news site with many articles about Princess Diana and the royal history.

### The Diana, Princess of Wales Memorial Fund
www.dianaprincessofwalesmemorialfund.org

Learn more about the Diana, Princess of Wales Memorial Fund and its charitable work.

### Princess Diana Remembered
www.princess-diana-remembered.com

Another fan site dedicated to Diana, this particular site has a comprehensive archive of Diana's wardrobe, including iconic outfits and accessories.

## Royal Fans

www.royal-fans.com

This fan website is a great resource to discover more about the modern royal family.

## Videos

### The History of Royal Wedding Souvenirs

www.bbc.com/news/business-13207012

A short BBC video special on the history of the royal wedding souvenir.

### Princess Diana Documentary

www.youtube.com/watch?v=KE5p2kiZWx8

This documentary on Princess Diana is chock full of interviews from experts and those who knew Diana best.

# BIBLIOGRAPHY

"1981: Prince Charles and Lady Di to Marry." BBC News. February 24, 1981. Accessed January 5, 2016. news.bbc. co.uk/onthisday/hi/dates/stories/february/24/news-id_2516000/2516759.stm.

"5 Mini-Disasters at Princess Diana's Wedding." The Royal Fans All About Royal Family. August 11, 2015. Accessed January 6, 2016. www.royal-fans.com/5-mini-disasters-at-princess-dianas-wedding/.

"AIDS Patients Now Living Longer, But Aging Faster." *NPR Health*. November 10, 2009.

Apple, Jr., R.W. "Amid Splendor, Charles Weds Diana." *New York Times*, July 29, 1981.

"Back Off, Queen Tells Press." *Montreal Gazette*, January 4, 1984.

Brown, Tina. *The Diana Chronicles*. New York, New York, NY: Broadway Books, 2008. 69.

Clayton, Tim and Phil Craig. *Diana: Story of a Princess*. New York, NY: Simon and Schuster, 2013.

"Diana Falls Down the Stairs." *Daily Mail*, February 8, 1982.

"Diana, Princess of Wales." *Telegraph*, August 31, 1997. Accessed January 12, 2016. www.telegraph.co.uk/news/obituaries/royalty-obituaries/1542104/Diana-Princess-of-Wales.html

"Diana, Princess of Wales." The Leprosy Mission of England and Wales. Accessed January 6, 2016. www.leprosymission. org.uk/about-us-and-leprosy/our-history/diana-princess-of-wales.aspx.

"Diana - Princess of Wales Full Biography," YouTube video, 3:12:51, posted by Paulo Carvalho, May 24, 2013, www.youtube.com/watch?v=KE5p2kiZWx8.

"Diana, Princess of Wales: Frequently Asked Questions." Diana, Princess of Wales. Accessed January 6, 2016. www.dianapow.com/faq.html.

Early, Chas. "June 21, 1982: A Future King Arrives as Princess Diana Gives Birth to Prince William." BT.com. June 21, 2015. Accessed January 6, 2016. home.bt.com/news/world-news/june-21-1982-a-future-king-arrives-as-princess-diana-gives-birth-to-prince-william-11363987656319.

"Engagement." Princess-Diana.com. Accessed January 6, 2016. www.princess-diana.com/diana/engagement.htm.

Goldman, John. "7-Year-Old AIDS Patient Shares Hug With Princess." *Los Angeles Times*, February 4, 1989.

"Hello, Harry!" *People*, October 1, 1984.

Hicks, India. "Princess Margaret in Her Nightie, Sweets from the Queen of Tonga and Diana Singing Just One Cornetto! A Royal Bridesmaid's VERY Surprising Big Day." *Daily Mail Online.* January 7, 2011. Accessed January 5, 2016. www.dailymail.co.uk/femail/article-1345229/Royal-wedding-India-Hicks-bridesmaid-memories-Prince-Charles-Dianas-wedding.html.

"Humanitarian Work." The Diana, Princess of Wales Memorial Fund. Accessed January 6, 2016. www.dianaprincessof-walesmemorialfund.org/humanitarian-work.

Katz, Gregory. "Prince Charles Seems like the Forgotten Man | Toronto Star." Thestar.com. March 7, 2011. Accessed January 6, 2016. www.thestar.com/news/world/royals/2011/03/07/prince_charles_seems_like_the_forgotten_man.html.

Kelley, Kitty. *The Royals*. New York, New York, NY: Grand Central Pub., 2010.

Kitzinger, Sheila. "Princess Diana Gave Birth to Wills Standing up as Charles Held Her, Reveals Natural Childbirth Activist Sheila Kitzinger Who Advised Lindo Wing Ahead of Royal Birth." *Daily Mail Online.* May 1, 2015. Accessed January 6, 2016. www.dailymail.co.uk/femail/article-3064807/Princess-Diana-gave-birth-Wills-standing-Charles-held-reveals-natural-childbirth-activist-SHEILA-KITZINGER-advised-Lindo-wing-ahead-royal-birth.html.

"Laundry Lady Diana's Early Years to Be Revealed in New Book by Prince William." Princess Diana News. August 29, 2007. Accessed January 6, 2016. dianaremembered.wordpress.com/page/102/.

"Listening to the roars, Diana said to her husband: "They want us to kiss." The Royal Fans: All About Royal Family. December 31, 2015. Accessed January 6, 2016. www.royal-fans.com/listening-to-the-roars-diana-said-to-her-husband-they-want-us-to-kiss/.

Mallick, Heather. "The Princess and the Press." *Toronto Sun*, October 19, 1997.

"Mandela and Diana Charities Join Forces." *BBC News*. November 2, 2002. Accessed January 6, 2016. news.bbc.co.uk/2/hi/uk_news/2392637.stm.

"The Man Who Will Be King." *Time*, May 15, 1978, p. 8.

Mattern, Joanne. *Princess Diana*. New York, NY: DK Publishing, 2006.

McDowell, Colin. *Diana Style*. New York, NY: St. Martin's Press, 2007.

Morris, Kelly. "Bulimia: The Princess Diana Eating Disorder." *Mirror Mirror*. 2007. Accessed January 6, 2016. www.mirror-mirror.org/princess-diana-eating-disorder.htm.

"On the Trail of London's Sloane Rangers." *New York Times*, March 25, 1985.

Opie, Robert. "The History of Royal Wedding Souvenirs," *BBC Video*, 3:31, April 27, 2011. Accessed January 12, 2016. www.bbc.com/news/business-13207012.

"Princess Diana's Childhood." Princess-Diana.com. Accessed January 6, 2016. www.princess-diana.com/diana/childhood.htm.

"Princess Diana's Dress Worn on First Official Appearance to Be Sold." *Telegraph*, April 12, 2010.

"Princess of Wales Diana Biography." *Encyclopedia of World Biography*. Accessed January 12, 2016. www.notablebiographies.com/De-Du/Diana-Princess-of-Wales.html

"Queen Heads List of Guests At Wedding." *The Montreal Gazette*, June 2, 1954.

"The Queen's Message." Buckingham Palace, Westminster. September 9, 1997. Accessed January 12, 2016. www.royal.gov.uk/HistoryoftheMonarchy/The%20House%20of%20Windsor%20from%201952/DianaPrincessofWales/TheQueensmessage.aspx.

Robertson, Mary. *The Diana I Knew*. New York, NY: Cliff Street Books, 1998.

Ross, Deborah. "Interview: Andrew Morton: He Couldn't Shout: `Diana Was in on This.'`She Trusted Me. It Would Have Been a Betrayal.'" *The Independent*, November 30, 1997.

Silverman, Stephen. "Prince William's Birth Was Induced." *People*, July 19, 2013.

Smith, Ron F. *Ethics in Journalism*. 6th ed. Malden, MA: Blackwell Pub., 2008.

"The Story Behind Diana's Secret Tapes." *NBC News*. March 4, 2004. Accessed January 12, 2016. www.nbcnews.com/id/4443363/ns/msnbc-deborah_norville_tonight/t/story-behind-princess-dianas-secret-tapes/#.VpVp6JMrK8o

"The 1980s AIDS Campaign." *BBC News*. October 16, 2005. Accessed January 6, 2016. news.bbc.co.uk/2/hi/programmes/panorama/4348096.stm.

"Viscount Althorp & The Hon. Frances Roche's Wedding." *The Royal Post*. June 11, 2012. Accessed January 6, 2016. theroyalpost.com/2012/06/11/viscount-spencer-the-hon-frances-roches-wedding/.

Wallace, Rob. "'Rebel Royal Mum': Diana's Legacy as Parent." *ABC News*. May 26, 2013. Accessed January 6, 2016. bcnews.go.com/International/rebel-royal-mum-dianas-legacy-parent/story?id=19241646.

Waller Rogers, Lisa. "Princess Diana: F & G." *Lisa's History Room*. July 21, 2010. Accessed January 6, 2016. lisawallerrogers.com/2010/07/21/princess-diana-f-and-g/.

"Women's History – Elizabeth Mallet." TYCI RSS. October 14, 2013. Accessed January 6, 2016. www.tyci.org.uk/wordpress/womens-history-elizabeth-mallet/.

# INDEX

Page numbers in **boldface** are illustrations. Entries in **boldface** are glossary terms.

# ABOUT THE AUTHOR

**Constance Beauregarde** was born in Beaver Dam, Wisconsin. She loves to write about princesses, fairy tales, and military history.